BIRTHING THE CHURCH

Dedication

To the elders of Cornerstone and their wives:

Mike and Karen Gerken for standing faithfully by us in the darkest, loneliest times.

Cliff and Audrey Wagner for growing up in the fire.

Larry and Nancy Cron for pursuing wholeness at any cost.

Jeff and Sue Guyett for smiling when we couldn't.

Jim and Marcia Tiffany for arguing supportively with me in all the right places.

BIRTHING THE CHURCH
Life-producing Principles of Church Growth
R. LOREN SANDFORD

Bridge Publishing, Inc.
Publishers of:
LOGOS • HAVEN • OPEN SCROLL

Birthing the Church

Copyright © 1984 by R. Loren Sandford
All rights reserved
Printed in the United States of America
International Standard Book Number: 0-88270-564-4
Library of Congress Catalog Card Number: 84-70054
Bridge Publishing, Inc.
South Plainfield, NJ 07080

Table of Contents

	Introduction	vii
1	Blessed Defeat	1
2	Speaking the Truth in Love	15
3	Reconciled to Disunity	33
4	"Loaves and Fishes"	49
5	A Theology for Unity	59
6	Worship	65
7	The Corporate Body	75
8	The Problem of Home Fellowships	83
9	Family and Church: A Biblical Balance	105
10	Burden Bearing	117
11	Pentecost Power	127

Introduction

Birthing the Church is actually teaching hung on the framework of a biography of the first years of an actual congregation. Admittedly, it is the story as seen through the eyes of its pastor, me. I make no claim to the final word on what happened to our church in those early days, but I maintain that what I relate is accurate to the best of my ability to discern.

This is a book about the sovereignty and grace of God as He is able to snatch victory from defeat, to transform disgrace into honor, to create cleanliness from filth, and to make possible life from death. In recent years the body of Christ has heard too much, I think, about victory. We think somewhat too exclusively in terms of the obviously good or successful side of things. I personally have hungered for someone to tell a success story with some good ol' blood and guts in it. Too often we have told the story of Christian joy without also telling of the suffering of the cross that frequently preceded it. It seems to me that Israel's victories in Scripture came in spite of and often through adversity. I have sought to reveal the adversities in order to lay greater stress on God's Word and sovereignty.

Therefore, in telling of our glories I have made no attempt to cover our multitudinous warts and wrinkles. I have poured my heart into the work, withholding nothing. I hope that in the process I have not unjustly represented anyone. Although no names are mentioned some may recognize their own stories in a less than flattering light. For this I apologize. I know of no way to relate the history in an honest and unsugar-coated manner without running the risk of offense. Not to tell of certain painful incidents would be to weaken the impact of the lessons we learned in living through those events. All those incidents, though painful, today have become a part of the wonder of our church which we call Cornerstone. I expect that every congregation, no matter what it knows in its collective head, will need to have some of its lessons written on its collective heart via painful episodes. Yet, perhaps through reading an unabashed account of victory *and* defeat, others will be able to avoid some of those painful situations themselves. At the very least, some may take comfort in seeing themselves reflected in these pages.

    The story told and the lessons learned cover a period of about two-and-a-half years from our opening to the completion of the book. This does not sound like a long time, but to all of us who lived the fiery intensity of the experience it seemed an eternity. I am reminded that Jesus and the disciples had a scant three years together, but it made a lifetime of difference. God has a timetable and a plan for every body of Christ. Ours was compressed because that was appropriate to us. Others who seek the same ends may be allotted mercifully longer periods of time. In either case, may the reader glean from these pages something of value to the pilgrimage of his own local body.

1
Blessed Defeat

Neal Neuenberg, senior pastor at Hope United Methodist Church in Sacramento, California, was the fifth senior pastor under whom I had served in five years at two churches, and we had an excellent working relationship, despite our very different personalities and approaches to ministry. What we had in common was a consuming drive to achieve and a godly passion for the expansion of the work through the laity. That kept Neal skinny and finally ruined my health.

One day about four-and-a-half months before I was scheduled to leave Hope, Neal and I faced each other across his desk. He was asking me disconcerting questions about the personnel I was preparing to leave in charge of my programs after my departure. To make matters worse, he kept interspersing (with a smile) all the reasons it would behoove me to stay on at Hope.

Suddenly, as he was speaking, a sharp pain stabbed at my heart, which skipped two beats and then stabilized. Nausea and shortness of breath followed. I collected myself and hid it from Neal.

Birthing the Church

I'd been getting sicker for months. More and more frequently I had to spend one or two days in bed, and I also suffered a couple of late evening dizzy spells with accompanying cold sweats and momentary blindness. A series of medical tests had revealed nothing, so that I had tabled my search for the source of the problem and pushed on in my characteristic workaholic fashion.

The experience in Neal's office frightened me, though, and so I sought unconventional help. Under the care of a naturopathic physician I discovered that the source of my problem was too many years of too much tension and not enough sleep, which—together with what might be called a prolonged overdose of junk food consumed in the favorite haunts of those youth to whom I was called to minister—had seriously polluted my body. Over the next few months a strict diet of natural foods and megavitamins began to remedy the problem.

Though feeling better physically, I nevertheless left Sacramento in January 1979 in a state of near emotional bankruptcy, burned out on pastoring and expecting not to serve in that capacity again. But I was not leaving the ministry. Beth and I were returning home to northern Idaho where I was to assume a position as Director of Elijah House together with my father. Elijah House is a non-denominational ministry dedicated to the restoration of the Christian family, the church, and the prophetic office according to Malachi 4:5-6 and Matthew 17:11. There I would do personal counseling and travel the country teaching churches, parachurch groups, and professional seminars on what boiled down to Christian family, Christian counseling, and charismatic concerns.

I was also to work with the Elijah House fellowship,

then basically a support group attached to the ministry. It was a step up of the sort men usually make when in their forties—and then only after long and very successful pastoral ministries. I was twenty-seven and only three years out of seminary, but I was destined to do this ministry very well in most respects.

The ministry in Sacramento had been most fruitful. In that crucible I organized and refined material on the Holy Spirit, counseling, leadership training, and a theology of worship which would serve me well in years to come. Every program in which I was involved showed major growth in the two-and-a-half years Beth (my wife) and I spent there. Many, many lives were changed.

My problem with tension in Sacramento had been a serious case of performance orientation. Performance orientation is when one confuses lovability and acceptability with achievement or behavior. It drove me to overtax myself physically while I fried internally in excess adrenalin. I carried every broken life tightly in my heart, and I took it as a personal failure if every problem could not be straightened out by my direct intervention. Just one negative reaction to a sermon or study was sufficient to wipe out a whole chorus of praise and send me into an emotional tailspin. In the end I simply burned out and God mercifully moved me on, which had been His plan all along.

I had asked the Lord to cure me of performance orientation, to let perfect love cast out fear (1 John 4:18) and set me free. At the bottom, where at last I was unable to perform, God was able to pour forth His love freely, and a healing began.

I remember January 7, 1979, as the date of our

Birthing the Church

going-away party from Sacramento. The church was packed. Beth and I were roasted by our friends and we laughed until we hurt. Then the praise came and I found my heart truly receiving for the first time. It ended with a song written for Beth and me by my friend, Karl Renschler, and his friend, Michael Sites. I do not remember the words anymore, but I do remember that the two of them sat directly in front of us and sang as though no one else were present. I finally lost it all together and sobbed deep, wracking sobs right in front of everyone. It was the beginning of healing. I had been reduced to a level where I could not perform, and found I was loved after all. But I still was not ready to take on another position in a local church. That was a hard spot in my heart.

My view of what was to come in Elijah House was that I could hit and run. Let me trouble-shoot a counselee, then send him back to be his pastor's headache as the healing worked itself out in real life. Let Beth and me walk into a local church with an armful of spiritual tools to deliver. Then let that local pastor struggle with the fallout as people fought to use them. We were most successful in these two aspects of the ministry and enjoyed the accolades of praise as we traveled the country.

Elijah House, itself, was painful, and I was to find myself feeling more broken and defeated than I had ever dreamed possible. It was the first time my ministerial touch had not borne almost instant gold. It was for me what is sometimes called the long, dark night of the soul. It lasted the two years that I served Elijah House and then through the first year of our new church's existence.

The long dark night is that time, sent by God, when nothing seems to succeed, when you don't seem to know

Blessed Defeat

what you know any longer. The Lord seems far off and nothing that used to work to bring on the sense of His presence seems to yield fruit anymore. Dark, thick despair wells up from deep within. It is the time of Psalm 22, "My God, my God, why hast Thou forsaken me? Far from my deliverance are the words of my groaning. O my God, I cry by day, but Thou dost not answer; And by night, but I have no rest . . . I am a worm, and not a man." Yet you determine to walk in obedience because God is God, His Word is law, and there are no alternatives.

It is a time which can only be understood by those who have lived it. While in the midst of it, you want to die, but afterward the experience is cherished as a gift. Something has changed in the inner man. Job described it best when he said, "I have declared that which I did not understand, things too wonderful for me, which I did not know . . . . I have heard of Thee by the hearing of the ear; but now my eye sees Thee; Therefore I retract, And I repent in dust and ashes" (Job 42:3-6). Job was a man already, "blameless, upright, fearing God, and turning away from evil" (1:1), but after the long, dark night of despair he came to a God-given understanding no mere man can grant or express. Perhaps in the profoundest sense, it was that he no longer had God, but God had him. He had thought himself to be spiritually rich, but God revealed to him his poverty.

During that time of darkness I was forced to search deeply in the inner man. I found a nauseating pit of pride and arrogance, and so I sought to know compassion. I had always been aware that I had been granted tools many other men had not. I had a basic wholeness, aside from performance orientation, which had enabled me to progress where others had been stymied. I had been given insights that many others had not seen. I had been given an inner strength that carried me where others failed. These were gifts of grace. They also blinded me to the plight of the poor in spirit. Job was shown his poverty. Just so, I was made to embrace mine. Thus a Pharisee became a disciple.

I see it now, albeit inadequately, as the time of blessed defeat. Let me explain what I mean, because "blessed defeat" is crucial to the story of our church, and because "defeat" is not a fashionable word for Christians to use these days.

It begins with a definition of the essence of sin. Sin is *the effort to take by force what God would give by grace.* The temptation to Eve in Genesis 3 was to eat of the fruit of the tree of the knowledge of good and evil so that she would be like God. The trouble was that she, together with Adam, was already like God, created in His image according to Genesis 1:26-27! God had given it by grace, but they reached out to take it by force. Virtually every mess we make in life is made because we don't believe God will give to us what is good just because He loves us, so we move to take it by our own hand and by our own method in our own time.

Dopers do drugs in order to take by force the high they don't believe God will give by grace. Thieves steal in order to attain the wealth and provision they don't believe our loving Lord will give. The sexual offender (adulterer, fornicator, homosexual, rapist) would take by force the delight and the fulfillment God would give within the law as a gift. My wife, Beth, was reared in a family in which the men could not be relied upon to demonstrate love and affection. When we were married, therefore, it was impossible for her to believe that God would bless her with affection from me, freely given, and so she set out to manipulate me to show her the affection she needed, i.e., to take by force the love God would give by grace. Of course, when she was manipulating to get it, then it was no longer my gift to her, and so it became the very last thing I wanted to give.

You see, the rule with us sinners is that, when we reach out to take the gift of grace (undeserved love) by an act of force, we lose it all. Adam and Eve reached out to be like God in knowing good and evil. By doing so they *became* evil and so became *un*like Him. The result was the loss of paradise and the shattering of every good relationship between God and man. Beth actually prevented me from showing the affection I wanted to show. The thief is thrown in jail. The doper becomes imprisoned by his drug so that the high becomes a hell. The sexual sinner, in seeking delight and fulfillment, actually dies in his ability to experience it.

Yet we persist. Since Adam, a "strong man" has been raised up in each of us, vested in self-preservation and self-advancement to take by force the gift of grace. A vast array of practices, habits and compulsions of the inner man are marshalled to accomplish this. I have practiced them all my life. They are all I know. They were forgiven when I came to Jesus, but they also need to be defeated. The strong man must die. "Therefore, consider the members of your earthly body as dead to immorality, impurity, passion, evil desire, and greed, which amounts to idolatry . . . since you *laid aside the old self with its*

Birthing the Church

evil practices, and have put on the new self who is being renewed to a true knowledge according to the image of the One who created him" (Col. 3:5-10). Galatians 2:20 puts it more forcefully: "I have been crucified with Christ; and it is no longer I who live, but Christ who lives in me . . . ." Before I can walk in the new, the old must die or be defeated.

While I was walking in my long dark night, the Lord made me aware that nearly every scriptural "great" had to be defeated before he could be truly effective. Each one was made to know the depth of his spiritual poverty. Paul was "advancing in Judaism beyond many of my contemporaries" (Gal. 1:14), busily seeking to earn the righteousness by act of man which the Lord Jesus was to give him by grace. He had to be struck down on the road to Damascus and temporarily blinded before he could receive. Such was his defeat.

Peter was ready the night before the crucifixion to die for the Lord in battle to establish the kingdom by force of arms. Jesus was on His way to establish that kingdom by a gracious act of sacrifice. Hours later Peter was denying the Lord three times. A defeated man, he went out and wept. Thereafter he was a much more usable disciple, able to preach a Pentecost sermon for the conversion of thousands and able to walk away from a flogging, "rejoicing that they had been considered worthy to suffer shame for His name" (Acts 5:41).

Abraham was promised a son. When the promise seemed impossible, he went out to establish God's promise of grace by his own act. Taking Hagar, his wife's maid, at his wife's urging, he fathered Ishmael whom God rejected. The promise would come by Sarah. Defeated

Blessed Defeat

and well past child-bearing years, Abraham and Sarah were granted Isaac, the son of promise by God's gift of undeserved love. Later, God asked him to sacrifice that son, to destroy all hope of ever seeing the promise fulfilled: "And I will make you a great nation, And I will bless you, And make your name great; And so you shall be a blessing; And I will bless those who bless you, And the one who curses you I will curse. And in you all the families of the earth shall be blessed" (Gen. 12:2-3). As he raised the knife, ready to slay his son and every dream with him, God stopped him and renewed the promise, yet with greater intensity: ". . . indeed I will greatly bless you, and I will greatly multiply your seed as the stars of the heavens, and as the sand which is on the seashore; and your seed shall possess the gate of their enemies. 'And in your seed all the nations of the earth shall be blessed, because you have obeyed My voice' " (22:17-18). By an act of obedience, which could have brought the final defeat of every hope, Abraham secured a greater promise. He would not hold on to the promise of God by force of his own act.

Jacob deserves a section all his own. Jacob was a twin. The promise given his mother (Gen. 25:23) was that two nations were in her womb, that one was stronger than the other, and that the older would serve the younger. Thereafter, Rebekah and Jacob the younger set out to make that promise a reality by acts of force, deceit and manipulation. It was to be the pattern of most of his life.

When his brother, Esau, came back famished from a time in the wilderness, Jacob took advantage of the momentary weakness in order to barter some food in exchange for his brother's birthright. A more significant

Birthing the Church

act of theft occurred when Rebekah overheard Isaac sending Esau out for some game with which to make his favorite stew, promising to bless him when he returned. Isaac was at the end of his life, nearly blind, seemingly diminished in his mental capacity, and so he was putting together a warm moment in which to pass his final blessing to his firstborn son. In Scripture the blessing of a father has real power to affect a life and so Jacob and Rebekah plotted to steal it. Jacob, dressed and scented as his brother, Esau, brought a stew. Isaac was fooled and Esau was enraged. Jacob, forced to flee, went to his father's kinsman, Laban. There the long process of defeat began as God, in love, could no longer permit him to go on forcing, and so ruining, the gift of grace.

Fleeing his home, Jacob laid down to sleep and had a dream in which God promised the land on which he lay for him and his descendants, who would be numerous beyond count and in whom all the families of the earth would be blessed (Gen. 28:10ff). Jacob, the snatcher of promises, as yet undefeated, tried a bargain to force the promise, "... *If* God will be with me and will keep me on this journey that I take, and will give me food to eat and garments to wear, and I return to my father's house in safety, *then* the Lord will be my God. And this stone, which I have set up as a pillar, will be God's house; and of all that Thou dost give me I will surely give a tenth to Thee" (Gen. 28:20-22).

He fell in love with Rachel, and served for her seven years. Laban gave him the homely Leah instead and made him serve seven more years for Rachel. Laban cheated him on wages and livestock repeatedly, and finally did everything he could to block Jacob's departure.

Blessed Defeat

No longer able to remain in the house of his father-in-law, and terrified of what his brother Esau might do, Jacob divided his company into two parts, hoping some remnant might survive the attack. That night "a man" came and wrestled with him until dawn. That "man," in a mystery, was the Lord. As they wrestled, Jacob's hip was dislocated. At dawn Jacob asked for a blessing and got one, a new name, Israel, meaning "the one who strives with God." It was a time of defeat, behind, before and in his relationship to God. Out of that defeat came reconciliation with Esau as a gift of grace, and later a renewal and intensification of the Abrahamic promises (Gen. 35:10-12). In the defeat of the strong man, grace is found.

Frequently when I pray for an alcoholic to be delivered he first gets worse. God must defeat him so that the strong man is broken. When I pray for a couple to stop arguing, they often first hit bottom so that the strong man defeats himself and grace follows. If I pray for one who must control everything around him, God sends a situation he cannot control so that defeat is the result. If I pray for a self-centered person, sometimes God will drive him so far into selfishness that the person himself is finally nauseated by it, and in defeat receives grace.

"Therefore, since Christ has suffered in the flesh, arm yourselves also with the same *purpose*, because he who has suffered in the flesh has ceased from sin," because the old man is defeated, "so as to live the rest of the time in the flesh no longer for the lusts of men," taking the gifts of God by force, "but for the will of God" (1 Pet. 4:1-2).

Always before, God had allowed me to push and shove my way to success. The success was actually His gift of grace, but He allowed the push and the shove and even

Birthing the Church

permitted me to think that my push and shove had won it. The long, dark night put an end to push and shove. I became a much more usable saint thereafter, and what is more, I could truly enjoy it. The fruit of the Spirit—love, joy, peace—came only after the power of the flesh had been defeated: "For if you are living according to the flesh, you must die; but if by the Spirit you are putting to death the deeds of the body, you will live" (Rom. 8:13).

The specific defeat which brought about the birth of the new church occurred in the Elijah House fellowship. For a little more than a year we tried to make it work as a supportive fellowship, one for another, as we met weekly for prayer, sharing and study. It didn't work. It had in years past, long before I came, but that day was over. Some of us were getting primary support from our local churches. The rest of us were asking Elijah House to provide that support and were angry that the others couldn't give it. The situation became intolerable, at least for me. I was responsible to make it work. On top of it all, my pastor's heart, which I was trying hard to ignore, was plainly and simply dying for lack of a congregation.

During this period, sometime in March 1980, I had one of those divinely powerful dreams. The most significant part of the dream was its ending. Beth and I had returned to the Sacramento church, just passing through. Neal, the senior pastor, used to stand on the right, just inside the door, to greet the people as they left the sanctuary. In this case he was outside on the left. When I came out he grasped both my hands in his and pleaded with great shuddering sobs for me to return to the church. He kept repeating the plea, and each time he did, a jolt of divine power would tug at my heart.

Blessed Defeat

At almost the same time, Bruce Austin, then President of Elijah House, had a dream in which he saw a church in a valley and a great storm raging all around it. He, Beth and I were being blown in from one side, and a great crowd of people were being driven in from the other.

The implications of both dreams became clear one night in late March. There had been some pretty nasty fireworks at a couple of Elijah House meetings. Bruce, my father and I met to discuss where we were going and what God might be saying to us in the turmoil. It became apparent that we were trying to meet needs that only a church could meet. Beyond that, we were teaching all across the country that every believer needs to be deeply connected to a local church, yet as a ministry we were connected to none, sent out by none. We were involved in varying degrees in our local churches, but as a corporation we were lacking the spiritual cover only a local church could provide. In the end, very few Elijah House members would be involved in Cornerstone's opening, but it was out of this malaise that it grew. In the midst of human defeat, God does His work of grace. Elijah House itself became what God had intended all along, a working body for the functioning and support of a ministry. Weekly meetings would not be necessary, fellowship would be a fruit of working together, and not a primary goal.

I still was not convinced. I asked God for a *minyan* unsolicited by me. A *minyan* is a quorum of ten required for the formation of a synagogue in Jewish tradition. He gave me seventeen who became our charter members in the months of planning that followed. Less than half were still with us a year later. Most of them cut us up

Birthing the Church

before they left. With the new entity was raised up a new strong man who needed new defeat to pave the way for grace. Every dream of glory, every call of God received and confirmed, was defeated in us before it was granted. It had to be His church, not ours, and He would see to it.

2
Speaking the Truth in Love

Further confirmation that we should open a church came when I found out the denomination through which I held my ordination was considering starting a new church in Post Falls (where I lived). In a flurry of excitement I drew up a lengthy proposal and rushed it off to the Church and Ministry Committee of the Washington North Idaho Conference of the United Church of Christ. I outlined the need for a mainline denominational charismatic fellowship in the Spokane-Post Falls-Coeur d'Alene area of Washington and Idaho, and asked if the denomination would like to sponsor such a new church. The reply indicated a lengthy institutional delay.

In subsequent discussions, the planning group and I decided to incorporate independently and then request affiliation with the denomination as an established congregation. This procedure was quicker and involved no denominational subsidy, which of course, gave us more freedom.

God had given me the name in early 1979, just a few months after leaving Sacramento. He was sneaky about

Birthing the Church

it. I wasn't ready even to consider returning to the pastorate, so He gave the name to me in the form of a careless thought: "If I were ever to open a church, 'Cornerstone' would be a good name." Today it serves as a reminder to us that the church is the Lord's and that it is a household in which He is the foundation. Planning meetings began in March of 1980. By mid-summer we had a constitution and were legally incorporated. August 17 we held our first service of worship in empty office space at Idaho Business Center in Post Falls. We packed it out. I had expected a crowd of curiosity seekers to come and go. They did. We opened with ninety adults in attendance and were down to thirty just a month later. From there we grew.

We wanted to affiliate with a denomination for many reasons. Most important to me was the element of check and balance. Too many independent congregations have gone off balance and into delusion because there was no wider body to question and confront. "Where there is no guidance, the people fall, But in abundance of counselors there is victory" (Prov. 11:14). The United Church of Christ is very liberal theologically while we, as a local congregation would be very conservative. We needed to face the question such a relationship raises lest we become narrow and shallow in our thinking and in our spirituality. If the denomination is off balance with the social gospel, then perhaps in having to grapple with that we would be reminded that there is more to the gospel than narrow fundamentalism. Perhaps the denomination would in turn listen to us about the primacy of the Word of God and the need for transformation to begin in the hearts of men. Then all would be edified.

Speaking the Truth in Love

Another reason for affiliating was that we felt we needed the spiritual cover which comes from being under authority. Ephesians 5:21 directs us to submit to one another out of reverence for Christ. There was a value and a protection in doing that corporately.

We felt we could have a wider impact for parish renewal as part of a denomination. A growing number of churches in the United Church of Christ are in renewal, but I believe we were unique in being founded already in renewal, specifically to be charismatic and evangelical. That put us in a kind of spotlight and gave great opportunity to witness to the power of the Spirit in our congregational life in circles beyond the borders of our local parish. We live in a time when many are leaving, rather than joining, the denomination. They do this because they are disgruntled with mainline denominational liberalism. We believe that Christ has called us to be a light in what is often a dark place. Christ has called us to illuminate the darkness, not leave it, and to seek the lost, not abandon them.

Beyond all that, I found I could not in good conscience leave the United Church to serve an independent congregation and still maintain my credibility in teaching that charismatics need to remain in their local churches and work for renewal. Had we not gone ahead with affiliation, I would have been forced to resign.

In our congregational system of government, our request to affiliate with the denomination required a congregational vote. By the time the vote was taken, we had twenty-five members, eight more than we started with. Of those eight new members, six opposed the move toward the denomination. It turned into our first major

Birthing the Church

argument. It was the first evidence of a sickness in some of our people which would rend the fabric of our fellowship again and again. It was not simply that they disagreed. Disagreement is necessary to the health of any group. Loving disagreement spells part of the difference between cultism and genuine faith. The issue was control. If the rest of us did not agree with this group, then we were not "hearing" them. It was inconceivable that we could hear and yet fail to go along. It was the beginning of months of quiet back-biting and undermining of the whole authority structure of the church from elders board to congregational vote.

When the vote was finally taken, only one voted against affiliation, but the damage had already been done. Our unity had been fractured, and it was never more than cosmetically restored until much later.

The denomination received us with open arms. Just a few years before this, the atmosphere in the UCC toward evangelicals and charismatics was openly hostile, but by 1980 a new spirit of "theological pluralism" had taken hold and a new openness was in vogue. It didn't necessarily mean that anyone had changed his mind theologically. It was just that the name calling had ceased and we were working hard to love one another.

I have heard us referred to as a "test case" in our conference to see if it is possible for a congregation such as ours to fit into a structure like the UCC where the predominant theology and style of worship is so different. My heart tells me that many of my colleagues don't quite regard us as legitimately UCC, but we are accepted, if not loved.

Speaking the Truth in Love

For our part, we support the programs and pronouncements we can, and we ignore the rest. Sometimes it isn't easy. The time may come when the denomination goes too far for us in some action or pronouncement and we would be forced to withdraw, but that time is not yet.

I can think of no adequate way to describe the many battles we fought that first year. My best hope is to convey the essential lessons the Lord lovingly and patiently burned into our hearts.

Ephesians 5:23 says that the husband is the head of the wife as Christ is the head of the church. We found that in every instance in which we allowed a woman to serve when she and her husband were not in proper submission to one another, lives were scarred and the fellowship weakened. We now watch to see who leads in a home. We watch to see if a man is able to do what he knows God has called him to do and what the eternal Word of God says he must do no matter how his wife feels about it. If he can, then God can use him in leadership. If he can't, then neither he nor his wife are fit. We watched again and again as the feelings of a wife ran amok, tearing up lives and hurting everyone, while the husband tagged along, justifying and excusing her behavior and in the end agreeing with her. "But if a man does not know how to manage his own household, how will he take care of the church of God?" (1 Tim. 3:5). Timothy is speaking of a particular kind of ego-strength by which a man heads his household and by which he lovingly contains and covers his family by righteous action in accord with God's Word. If he doesn't have it for the home, he won't have it for the church. In reality, the unchecked feelings of his wife will be the basis of his leadership decisions.

Birthing the Church

We learned not to let people into leadership until we knew why they had left their former churches, especially if there had been several prior involvements. Many came to us whose histories revealed patterns of undermining and criticizing authority until the atmosphere in the former churches became so intolerable that they had left voluntarily or had been driven out. Cornerstone was nearly destroyed by these unrepented judgments. More than half of our original leadership team left us before the end of the first full year. Many of these had torn up previous churches by dishonoring authority, and as a new congregation we had failed to examine the histories closely enough. We needed hands, and theirs were willing. The most common problem was an emotionally manipulative wife who bent and twisted every word and event in our congregational life to fit her judgments and fears. In such cases, ". . . she gave also to her husband with her, and he ate" (Gen. 3:6). Today we do leadership by the Book. It works. "And I shall make you pass under the rod, and I shall bring you into the bond of the covenant; and I shall purge from you the rebels and those who transgress against Me; I shall bring them out of the land where they sojourn, but they will not enter the land of Israel. Thus you will know that I am the Lord" (Ezek. 20:37-38).

The lesson we are still working on is the need for confrontation on the scriptural pattern. We paid a high price our first year for failing to understand and implement God's Word in this regard. In fact, I am not aware of a church anywhere which is not paying the price to some degree for failure to implement this aspect of the Law.

Speaking the Truth in Love

Matthew 18:15-17 says:

> And if your brother sins, go and reprove him in private; if he listens to you, you have won your brother. But if he does not listen to you, take one or two more with you, so that BY THE MOUTH OF TWO OR THREE WITNESSES EVERY FACT MAY BE CONFIRMED. And if he refuses to listen to them, tell it to the church; and if he refuses to listen even to the church, let him be to you as a Gentile and a tax-gatherer.

The Book of Proverbs is a compendium of notes on how to succeed. It says, "Drive out the scoffer, and contention will go out, Even strife and dishonor will cease" (Prov. 22:10).

We don't follow that advice often enough in our churches. If we did, more contentious Christians would be forced to deal with their sin and perhaps be delivered. That would be mercy. If we followed that advice, the very least that would occur would be that wolves would depart and cease eating sheep. That, too, would be mercy.

On this issue, balance between legalism, judgment and the requirement of love is found in the quality of repentance. ". . . If your brother sins, rebuke him; and if he repents, forgive him. And if he sins against you seven times a day, and returns to you seven times, saying, 'I repent,' forgive him" (Luke 17:3-4). We don't enforce expulsion for failure to perform but for failure to repent. If a brother or sister cannot see the sin and repent of it, then destruction to other members of the body and to the whole cause of Christ continues. "It is inevitable that stumbling blocks should come, but woe to him through whom they come! It would be better for him if a millstone were hung around his neck and he were thrown into the sea, than that he should cause one of these little ones to stumble" (Luke 17:1-2). When that group left we hurt, but we grew and the whole spirit of the church changed.

In enforcing an expulsion we are simply facing the reality of the destructiveness of sin. The hard requirement of love is that we face sin and deal with it so that lives are restored and protected. Repentance must involve a real change of heart. At this point, we are past questions of unconditional love, acceptance and forgiveness, and are dealing honestly with the fact that when someone is unwilling to see his sin and repent of it by taking steps to correct it, then situations repeat themselves and lives are again destroyed. The result of such a situation most certainly is *not* love. Love edifies.

In late March 1982 I asked the congregation three questions:

1. Would we rather *be* church than *play* church?
2. Would we rather have conflict with genuine love than peace with superficial or surface love?
3. If we were forced to choose between growth in the Lord with pain, and comfortable, peaceful stagnation, which would be it?

I asked the questions at a time when some rapid spiritual and numerical growth was occurring. At times like that the moments of decision come more quickly. We

Speaking the Truth in Love

were facing such a moment and it related directly to the questions. Ephesians 4 expressed the heart of it: "But speaking the truth in love, we are to grow up in all aspects into Him, who is the head, even Christ, from whom the whole body, being fitted and held together by that which every joint supplies, according to the proper working of each individual part, causes the growth of the body for the building up of itself in love" (Eph. 4:15-16). Again it says, "... SPEAK TRUTH, EACH ONE OF YOU, WITH HIS NEIGHBOR, for we are members of one another" (Eph. 4:25), and again, "Let no unwholesome word proceed from your mouth, but only such a word as is good for edification according to the need of the moment, that it may give grace to those who hear" (Eph. 4:29).

I then took an inventory of where we were in relation to this critical chapter. I found that we were well-equipped (Eph. 4:12) in many ways. A blessedly large number of us were skilled in basic principles of Christian counseling. We had a large number, not only of solo and ensemble musicians to fuel our concert ministry but also a significant group of gifted composers as well. Good leaders were in charge of our home fellowships. The children's ministries were in very capable hands. The list went on and on. As a result, we were doing quite well in the work of service so that the body had really begun to grow (Eph. 4:12). All of this had led to the unity spoken of in verse 13. In fact, our unity was better than at any time since we had opened. As the Word promises, the result was changed lives. More of us were becoming more profoundly Christ-like (Eph. 4:13, 15). This, at least, had produced a certain stability (Eph. 4:14). The turmoil of

Birthing the Church

our first year had led some to describe it as a ride on the Cornerstone roller coaster. The roller coaster was gone and, with it, the terrible fear that the whole thing could blow up again at any minute. We had scarcely been able to enjoy the highs for fear of the devastating lows we knew would come.

The crossroads we faced was the last step in the Ephesians sequence. From verse 15 we needed to learn to speak the truth in love. As time has passed, I have become more and more convinced that the bulk of pastoral equipping has to be done in the area of learning to speak the truth. The key to maturity and true Christ-likeness is, ultimately, the ability to speak the truth in love.

One might ask, "Which truth?" The first truth is obviously proclamation of the basic gospel. That, however, is easy. Any babe in the Lord can do it, and, in fact, babes do it best. They are still too excited to keep quiet! The second truth is the word of encouragement, affirmation or compliment. That, too, is relatively simple. The decision for maturity comes with the third and fourth truths, that of confrontation and correction, and that of confession.

One Friday night, during that same period of time, our elders' home fellowship met with a bundle of needs to share, fears to reveal, sins to be laid before the group in confession, and admonitions to be delivered. We responded to all this by beating around the bush, tantalizing one another with hints, and doing nothing. In the end, we all smiled at one another and went home angry! Our congregation was not speaking truth to one another in love because the leaders were not doing it among themselves.

Speaking the Truth in Love

"Speaking the truth," in the Greek of the New Testament, is a one-word derivative of *aletheia,* which means, "the real or actual state of affairs." To speak the truth, therefore, is to speak the real state of affairs as it is in my heart, in your heart, in your effect on people, in your attitude, in your actions, in the Word of God, and so on. To do so "in love" means that the goal of such speaking is the edification, upbuilding, strengthening and maturing of another person or of the body of Christ at large. By contrast, most of us speak the truth in self-defense and/or self-offense with predictably devastating results.

I sometimes do what I call, "The Gospel According to Practice," in order to make a point. The following perversion of the Word of God is a reflection of what our people were doing in March of 1982:

| Matthew 18:15-17: If your brother sins, go and tell the pastor, and if the pastor won't do what you want him to, then tell a friend. | *vs.* | And if your brother sins, go and reprove him in private; if he listens to you, you have won your brother. But if he does not listen to you, take one or two more with you, so that BY THE MOUTH OF TWO OR THREE WITNESSES EVERY FACT MAY BE CONFIRMED. And if he refuses to listen to them, tell it to the church; and if he refuses to listen even to the church, let him be to you as a Gentile and a tax-gatherer. |

Birthing the Church

Luke 17:3: If your brother sins, get the pastor to rebuke him.

vs.

... If your brother sins, rebuke him; and if he repents, forgive him.

1 Timothy 5:20: Those who continue in sin, discuss with others in their absence.

vs.

Those who continue in sin, rebuke in the presence of all, so that the rest may be fearful of sinning.

1 Thessalonians 5:14: We urge you brethren, be frustrated with the unruly, talk about the faint-hearted, criticize the weak, and expect perfection from all men.

vs.

And we urge you, brethren, admonish the unruly, encourage the faint-hearted, help the weak, be patient with all men.

Galatians 6:1: Brethren, even if a man is caught in any trespass, you who are spiritual ignore such a one in a spirit of gentleness.

vs.

Brethren, even if a man is caught in any trespass, you who are spiritual, restore such a one in a spirit of gentleness.

James 5:14: Is anyone among you sick? Let him hope that he gets well.

vs.

Is anyone among you sick? Let him call for the elders of the church, and let them pray over him, anointing him with oil in the name of the Lord.

James 5:16: Therefore, keep your sins to yourself so that you will not get hurt. The effective prayer of a righteous man might humiliate me.	*vs.*	Therefore, confess your sins to one another, and pray for one another, so that you may be healed. The effective prayer of a righteous man can accomplish much.
Colossians 3:16: Let the word of Christ richly dwell within you, with all wisdom teaching and admonishing one another silently in your hearts.	*vs.*	Let the word of Christ richly dwell within you, with all wisdom teaching and admonishing one another with psalms and hymns and spiritual songs, singing with thankfulness in your hearts to God.

    I finally told our people not to come to me with complaints until those involved had been confronted. If the confrontation didn't work, I would referee, or if advice was needed on how to confront, I would give it, but biblical procedure would have to be followed first. I was speaking from genuine desperation. Cornerstone wrote the book on "The Gospel According to Practice." Disunity comes not from what we do and say *to* one another so much as from what we do and say *about* one another. If my brother offends me, the relationship between us is polluted, but if I tell others about it, then the whole body is defiled. Talkers had nearly destroyed us. I would have to say that talkers were not very welcome at our church by March of 1982.

Birthing the Church

We all know John 3:16, "For God so loved the world, that He gave His only begotten Son, that whosoever believes in Him should not perish, but have eternal life." The thought is only completed, however, in John 3:20-21:

> For everyone who does evil hates the light, and does not come to the light, lest his deeds should be exposed. But he who practices the truth *comes to the light, that his deeds may be manifested* as having been wrought in God.

There is a need for transparency in our individual lives. We are called to submit ourselves *to one another* out of reverence for Christ (Eph. 5:21). As I work that word out in obedience to Christ, I open my life to my small group fellowship. As I lay my life before them, I submit myself for rebuke, encouragement, forgiveness, correction and edification, all in love. I have only one perspective on my life—mine—and it is a selfish, sinful one. I desperately need my brothers and sisters to speak the truth to me in love. They tell me when my work pace is costing me my humanity. They tell me when my fears are justified and when not. They tell me when I am carrying too much of the load in the church and rebuke me for not distributing it better. They tell me I am a good guy when I feel like a bad one. They point up my successes when I can't see them for myself.

> Let us hold fast the confession of our hope without wavering, for He who promised is faithful; and let us consider how to stimulate one another to love and good deeds, not forsaking

our own assembling together, as is the habit of some, but encouraging one another; and all the more as you see the day drawing near (Heb. 10:23-25).

Here is a special word of warning for those in leadership positions. "A fool's vexation is known at once, But a prudent man conceals dishonor" (Prov. 12:16). A leader must *not* share his innermost self with rank and file. Our culture has developed an insidious hatred for authority. Any leader who reveals himself carelessly will sooner or later see that revelation used against him. In our first year I made the mistake of revealing myself, my doubts, my fears, my hurts, and my inner struggles to some who should not have known. It was all used later as ammunition to attack and weaken me in my position as pastor. I now encourage my elders and other group leaders to encourage their group members to share openly among themselves, but to save the expression of their own innermost needs for our leaders' group. Let it be remembered that Jesus himself had an inner circle of twelve within which was an inner circle of three, and only the three accompanied Him to Gethsemane. Leadership can be a lonely role.

The word of rebuke needs a word of balance. Rebuke done in self-defense is not love, but rebuke for the other's sake leads to edification. More than that, I have found that when I am being rebuked, even if my brother is absolutely wrong, God has put something in it for me, even if it isn't contained in the words being spoken. In our first year I was under constant attack, being falsely accused of all manner of manipulation. It was 100

Birthing the Church

percent untrue, but the cumulative effect on me was the destruction of my over-active need to be approved by one and all. Because of that pressure, I am today a much less defensive person, and I am a good deal more content with not being a spiritual superman with an answer to every problem. I even find myself genuinely undisrupted when someone wants to leave our church. My detractors were dead wrong, but God used the pressure to deal in some other areas of my life. There was something there for me. Our Lord is that big! It is Romans 8:28 again, "And we know that God causes all things to work together for good to those who love God, to those who are called according to His purpose."

Another word of balance is that we must avoid making an idolatry of confrontation. Our focus must be on what God is doing and has done, rather than on what is not yet done. Sin will be plain enough and sufficiently damaging without giving it seventy-millimeter projection. One of my best friends in college was destroyed as a Christian leader by a group that was into challenging one another to be the best they could be for Christ. They lost sight of balance and he lost sight of hope.

I have often heard our people say, after a silent meeting of the home fellowship, that they didn't "feel led" to open up. My answer is that God's eternal Word supercedes any momentary leading of the Spirit, and it says, "But give that which is within as charity, and then all things are clean for you" (Luke 11:41). We may say we are fearful of being judged, but it won't be the truth. We are really only afraid of opening up and/or confronting because we are fearful of not being liked for it. That fear is childish, and we are speaking here of maturity.

Neither rebuke nor encouragement will mean instant change. The biblical injunction to confront with one, then two or more, and then with the church, I believe, is given to insure not only that damaging sin is expunged from the body, but to make certain we have done all we can to restore the sinner in love before expulsion. Let us go the second mile with one another before implementing the extremity of the law. I once said, "Let sinners be sinners," to one who was pressing me to act on an expulsion. He misunderstood and thought that I was unwilling to deal with sin. In reality, I was addressing his impatience and calling for a second mile of forbearance. I believe God calls us to that. Expulsion is for when the second mile avails nothing.

> You too be patient; strengthen your hearts, for the coming of the Lord is at hand. Do not complain, brethren, against one another, that you yourselves may not be judged; behold, the Judge is standing right at the door. As an example, brethren, of suffering and patience, take the prophets who spoke in the name of the Lord. Behold, we count those blessed who endured . . . (James 5:8-11).

Rebuke, confession and encouragement initiate a process of change and then sustain it over a period of time. Judgment begins when we forget the time element and demand that maturity occur immediately in its fullness. People take years, not days, weeks or months to work through brokenness. For example, the alcoholic is engaged in a life-long struggle with many stumblings before final deliverance. Selfish people become unselfish only piece by piece as God defeats the old nature and brings about a healthy disgust. Weak individuals, easily led into negativity, will be captivated and fall many times as wobbly knees gradually develop strength. One woman in our church, for example, had a habit of letting others catch her up in negativity. After a year she was still getting caught in it, but instead of seeing it a week later, she was seeing it moments later and repenting immediately. That was progress! It came slowly and painfully, but it was permanent and precious. Later on she licked it altogether. Our sin nature is stubborn. It does not want to die. No wonder the Word of God says so much about forbearance and patience! "Preach the word; be ready in season and out of season; reprove, rebuke, exhort, with great patience and instruction" (2 Tim. 4:2), speaking the truth in love, so that we "... grow up in all aspects into Him, who is the head, even Christ" (Eph. 4:15).

3
Reconciled to Disunity

"Reconciled to disunity" sounds a little strange. Out of all the trouble of our first year, perhaps the most significant personal thing I learned was to be reconciled to disunity as a means of maintaining true unity.

All my life growing up as a pastor's son, I had questioned why the church could not remain at peace. Cornerstone forced the issue for me. I searched the Word and uncovered some significant keys. Philippians 1:27 speaks of "standing firm in one spirit." An injunction to stand firm is only necessary where there is pressure to falter. Ephesians 4:2 is a command to walk "with all humility and gentleness, with patience, showing forbearance to one another in love." In Philippians, again, at 4:5, Paul commands the people to "let your forbearing spirit be known to all men." "And so, as those who have been chosen of God, holy and beloved, put on a heart of compassion, kindness, humility, gentleness and patience; bearing with one another, whoever has a complaint against anyone; just as the Lord forgave you, so also should you" (Col. 3:12-13). Paul ordered Titus "To malign no one, to be uncontentious, gentle, showing every consideration for all men" (Titus 3:2). James connected the need to cease complaining against one another with patience (James 5:9-10). Apparently the early church had some significant problems with unity, so much so that the idea of forbearance or patiently "putting up with one another" appears with distressing frequency in the pages of Scripture.

Seeing all of this helped, but what finally enabled me to cope with disunity was James 3:8. "But no one can tame the tongue; it is a restless evil and full of deadly poison."

I then began to look at what had been the carrier of the poisons which issued from the diseases I have mentioned before. I saw that the major sources of disunity were:

1. *The tongue.* The most common mechanism is simply repeating what has been heard when what has been heard is less than edifying or complimentary. Others are more subtle, like analyzing one another's problems when the one being analyzed is not present. We call that one "loving concern." Or we say, "Would you pray about this? I am just concerned," and in reality it's just a self-sanctified means of sharing negativity.

2. *Threatened egos.* We react badly to whatever is happening in the church most often because it reflects negatively on self or threatens self's position of importance. The most significant cause of my difficulty in handling crises was that my personal success

Reconciled to Disunity

was bound up in it. The result was that I was most ill-prepared to resolve it.

3. *The tongue.*

4. *Selfish ambition.* This is the practice of subtly, or not so subtly, manipulating others so that my pet project and I appear successful. As in number 2, I am using the church to support my sense of self-importance, usually at the expense of others. "Those who do not fall down and worship at the idol of my program, my position in the church or my sanctified picture of myself will be thrown into the fiery furnace of my righteous indignation heated seven times." It won't be long before a manipulator or self-exalter runs out of people who will cooperate. That's when the "noble martyr" surfaces. "After all I've done for this church ... I feel used!"

5. *The tongue.*

6. *False teaching.* Off-balance teaching always has the effect of shredding the fabric of the fellowship as history has well demonstrated. This can include outright heresy or simple over-emphasis on one point of doctrine or practice to the exclusion of those portions of the gospel which balance it.

7. *The tongue.*

8. *Misguided zeal.* This is the practice of putting too much pressure on folks too soon,

Birthing the Church

whether that means, for instance, asking babes in the Lord to have the faith skills of twenty-year veterans, of pressuring a congregation to look at a building program a year before God's time. It makes folks angry because it is compassionless and loveless and it violates persons. One mistake we almost made, but narrowly avoided, was to push hard for a land purchase too soon. We opened with such a bang that we were overwhelmed by the sheer press of numbers in the first few weeks. We lost our balance and ran off looking for land, dreaming big dreams. One courageous soul had the good courage to stand against the flow and speak God's word of restraint. We later found out that our talk of a land purchase had terrified a good portion of our fledgling congregation. Had we pursued the project then, we might have lost a good many members. I also was forced to take a faith inventory and found that our people were not as mature in the Lord as I had thought at first. Too many had no idea at all what I was asking and were feeling pushed and manipulated by the tone of my preaching. There was some push from me due to frustration, but certainly no manipulation. I was simply preaching over the heads of too large a portion of my congregation and it frightened them. I backed up and began again on a more basic level and we began to move forward together.

Reconciled to Disunity

9. *The tongue.*

10. *Unwillingness to forgive.* We can define this one as the harboring and nurturing of hurts. Forgiveness is not forgiveness until things are better than before and we are actually grateful for the hurt delivered because of what we learned. That's the effect of the cross of Christ.

11. *The tongue.*

12. *Idolatry.* I view this as a practice which occurs any time something other than Jesus and His glory consumes and fills my vision. Disagreement becomes disunity when all we can see is the trouble rather than the glory in the fellowship all around us.

13. *The tongue.*

My usual approach to disunity was to marshall all my tools of rebuke, pressure, exhortation and condemnation to enforce unity. It never worked. The church just became discouraged and everybody got tired. The key was that passage in James—that the tongue cannot be tamed. It is a restless evil, full of deadly poison, which cannot be fully conquered. As long as there is a church this side of the rapture, there will be talk, and where there is talk, there will be sin which leads to disunity. Yet Matthew says we'll drink deadly poison and not be harmed (Mark 16:18). We can therefore, absorb the poison of the tongue to a degree and not be damaged. If I am to preserve unity, then I must be reconciled to

Birthing the Church

disunity in the church as long as the church remains on earth. The parable of the wheat and the tares helped also. It clearly teaches that good and evil will be mixed in the church until the Lord returns for the harvest. Every church to which Paul wrote had a fight. That's why he wrote and those letters now comprise the better part of our New Testament. The disciples, walking in Jesus' very presence, had arguments. One of them betrayed Him to death. Each of those troubles had to involve the use of the tongue.

We did, however, discover some hard-nosed, "speaking the truth in love" principles that helped us in relation to the tongue—when to listen, when not to listen, when to speak, when not to speak, and so on. It begins with fruit inspection according to Matthew 7:17-20. No bad fruit ever comes from a good tree. The righteous mouth, even when speaking about negative things, will feed, strengthen and renew the heart. The wicked mouth will bear opposite fruit to steal joy and destroy true love. It bears no peace and lifts no burden. If the fruit of any speaker's words is freedom, hear him! But if the fruit of any speaker's words is heaviness and stolen joy, turn away!

> Proverbs 10:19-21
> When there are many words, transgression is
>   unavoidable,
> But he who restrains his lips is wise.
> The tongue of the righteous is as choice silver,
> The heart of the wicked is worth little.
> The lips of the righteous feed many,
> But fools die for lack of understanding.

Reconciled to Disunity

Proverbs 12:18-20
There is one who speaks rashly like the thrusts of a sword,
But the tongue of the wise brings healing.
Truthful lips will be established forever,
But a lying tongue is only for a moment.
Deceit is in the heart of those who devise evil,
But counselors of peace have joy.

Proverbs 15:2, 4
The tongue of the wise makes knowledge acceptable.
But the mouth of fools spouts folly.
A soothing tongue is a tree of life,
But perversion in it crushes the spirit.

Proverbs 17:4
An evildoer listens to wicked lips,
A liar pays attention to a destructive tongue.

Proverbs 18:20, 21
With the fruit of a man's mouth his stomach will be satisfied;
He will be satisfied with the product of his lips.
Death and life are in the power of the tongue,
And those who love it will eat its fruit.

Proverbs 21:23
He who guards his mouth and his tongue,
Guards his soul from troubles.

Proverbs 25:23
The north wind brings forth rain,
And a back-biting tongue, an angry countenance.

Birthing the Church

James 1:26
If anyone thinks himself to be religious, and yet does not bridle his tongue but deceives his own heart, this man's religion is worthless.

James 3:5-12
So also the tongue is a small part of the body, and yet it boasts of great things. Behold, how great a forest is set aflame by such a small fire! And the tongue is a fire, the very world of iniquity; the tongue is set among our members as that which defiles the entire body, and sets on fire the course of our life, and is set on fire by hell. For every species of beasts and birds, of reptiles and creatures of the sea, is tamed, and has been tamed by the human race. But no one can tame the tongue; it is a restless evil and full of deadly poison. With it we bless our Lord and Father; and with it we curse men, who have been made in the likeness of God; from the same mouth come both blessing and cursing. My brethren, these things ought not to be this way. Does a fountain send out from the same opening both fresh and bitter water? Can a fig tree, my brethren, produce olives, or a vine produce figs? Neither can salt water produce fresh.

Finally, Proverbs 26:20-28 is a key. It capsulizes all we learned about dealing with chronic poisonous mouths in our first two years.

Reconciled to Disunity

20) For lack of wood the fire goes out, And where there is no whisperer, contention quiets down.

21) Like charcoal to hot embers and wood to a fire, So is a contentious man to kindle strife.

22) The words of a whisperer are like dainty morsels, And they go down into the innermost parts of the body.

23) Like an earthen vessel overlaid with silver dross Are burning lips and a wicked heart.

24) He who hates disguises it with his lips, But he lays up deceit in his heart.

25) When he speaks graciously, do not believe him, For there are seven abominations in his heart.

26) Though his hatred covers itself with guile, His wickedness will be revealed before the assembly.

27) He who digs a pit will fall in it, And he who rolls a stone, it will come back on him.

28) A lying tongue hates those it crushes, And a flattering mouth works ruin.

There is a difference between the one who utters a wrong or negative word occasionally, but repents, and the one whose life yields consistently disruptive fruit as a result of the tongue. We have discovered that this sort of individual will not repent, but rather play the noble martyr when consistently stopped. So we examine the fruit of an individual's mouth, and if it is consistently to confuse and to damage other members of the flock, then we follow biblical procedure according to Matthew 18 to confront and eventually break fellowship when there is no repentance. According to Proverbs 26:20-28, this individual is characterized by the following:

1. He kindles strife and contention (verses 20-21). We ask a simple question for those who struggle with what they hear. "Were you upset *before* you listened?" God steals no joy; He is not the author of confusion.

2. He sounds good and gracious, but the end of his talk is destruction (verses 22 and 25). No matter how he sounded or how much "concern" or "love" he expressed, did you feel clean and edified at the end? Did his words, even if negative, *lift* a burden you had, or did they impose one? Were you stronger or freer as a result?

3. He will hide himself and refuse to admit that he's guilty of such talk (verses 24 and 26). When confronted he may say, "I'll pray about it, but I just don't see it." *Be ruthless about fruit inspection.* The second and third time smoke rises from the same spot in the forest, we must know that a fire burns there. In such cases only a fool accepts denial. Don't even accept a rational sounding explanation of what an individual's words were meant to convey when the fruit is consistently bad. Fruit tells all. Bad fruit can't come from a good tree.

4. He will claim love for the one talked about, but actually hates him (verses 24, 25, 26 and 28). The claim of love is intended to disarm the hearer in order to get him to swallow a bitter pill with a sugar-coating. Love *edifies*. That is the law. Don't accept a statement of love when the result is not edifying.

I once asked the Lord why tongues so persistently wag in the church. The answer He gave is that people need to feel important and if an individual can get a hold on some juicy bit of a problem or give an analysis of someone's life or condition, then he can feel that he is important and on the inside of things. For the individual who needs this sort of bolstering, repentance means giving up that false sense of importance and so implies a facing of the fear that, after all, he might be truly as insignificant as he's afraid he is. The reason we fail to confront this type of individual is much the same. We are afraid of the reaction, the possibility of rejection. Let us pray for the courage of obedience and for the inner security that comes from our relationship with Christ so that we can, indeed, lovingly confront the talker for his own healing and for the protection of the body of Christ.

The more I have observed the body of Christ, the more convinced I am that our number one enemy is not Satan but our mouths. How many of us would move into a home with a basement full of septic tank overflow? The stench would drive us out no matter how nice the home. Just so, how can we expect unbelievers to join us in our faith if our spiritual house stinks? It won't matter how attractive our programs and our worship may be. Talk sets up an atmosphere that outsiders feel, and it will bring church growth to a standstill. The absence of talk creates an aroma of peace which newcomers sense and to which they warm.

These are simple, but difficult lessons. Let us keep and faithfully practice them.

On the question of unity in general, how could the church *not* be full of hurtful situations and incidents? It's for sinners, not perfect people. It's a hospital for the spiritually sick, not a vacation spot. We come to church

Birthing the Church

not because we're good people, but because we're not such good people and we need help. No reputable hospital would keep all of its paranoics in the same room. They would kill one another! No hospital would place all the violent aggressives in one cell, untethered. But in both of these instances that is precisely the method of our Lord! To make it even more complicated in His looney bin, the moment you check in as a patient He makes you a doctor, or at least an intern! Read it. It is Ephesians 4, 1 Corinthians 12, and Romans 12! We are a bunch of crazy people trying to help a bunch of crazy people. With a plan like that, we ought to fire God and find another leader!

> For consider your calling, brethren, that there were not many wise according to the flesh, not many mighty, not many noble; but God has chosen the foolish things of this world to shame the wise, and God has chosen the weak things of the world to shame the things which are strong, and the base things of the world and the despised, God has chosen, the things that are not, that He might nullify the things that are, that no man should boast before God (1 Cor. 1:26-29).

The real miracle of the church is that it exists at all. The wonder of the church is that by God's grace it works so that men are, in fact, redeemed and changed. Further, if our churches are *not* full of the lost, the lame, the sick and the sinners, then we are failing the gospel.

We need to come to a point of trusting God enough to

let one another fail and to free one another to have misperceptions of each other. Not that we don't need to deal with sin, because we do, but we do not need to have a major crisis each time something strikes us wrongly. Let us believe Romans 8:28 and its implications: "And we know that God causes all things to work together for good to those who love God, to those who are called according to His purpose." We practice criticism of one another and of our leaders continually, in spite of the Lord's command by Paul's pen: "Finally, brethren, whatever is true, whatever is honorable, whatever is right, whatever is pure, whatever is lovely, whatever is of good repute, if there is any excellence and if anything worthy of praise, *let your mind dwell on those things"* (Phil. 4:8).

Sooner or later a child always criticized will be in rebellion, possibly for life, and will develop a less than edifying picture of himself. Praise, by contrast, enthrones God (Ps. 22:3) and calls His people to life. He chooses outcasts and sinners to be His leaders, knowing and expecting that they will fail. He has already planned for that and is able to accomplish His work in spite of, and even through, our weakness, "for power is perfected in weakness" (2 Cor. 12:9). We panic and fall into disunity only because we don't believe God. Because we don't believe Him, we are unable to see His hand at work in disaster.

"Forbearance" means "tolerance." God did not say that we were responsible to change one another. He said we should tolerate and put up with one another and so help one another to change. If we can keep that straight, we will keep the frustration level with one another down. Therefore, in that context, let us be reconciled to disunity.

Birthing the Church

Unity comes neither from performing, acting and saying rightly, nor from succeeding in all things, but from how we handle failure. We get in trouble because we base our happiness on a standard of performance rather than on grace. Thus every conflict or loose word appears to us as the end of the world. No one, if he truly knows Jesus, deliberately hurts anyone in the body of Christ, but it happens and it's unavoidable. Unity develops from the way in which we handle the woundings. Thank God for conflict! The strongest bonds are those tried by fire.

In sum: (1) Be reconciled to disunity. (2) Base unity not on right actions but on handling wrong ones in love.

Romans 12:9-21

Let love be without hypocrisy. Abhor what is evil; cling to what is good. Be devoted to one another in brotherly love; give preference to one another in honor; not lagging behind in diligence, fervent in spirit, serving the Lord; rejoicing in hope, persevering in tribulation, devoted to prayer, contributing to the needs of the saints, practicing hospitality. Bless those who persecute you; bless and curse not. Rejoice with those who rejoice, and weep with those who weep. Be of the same mind toward one another; do not be haughty in mind, but associate with the lowly. Do not be wise in your own estimation. Never pay back evil for evil to anyone. Respect what is right in the sight of all men. If possible, so far as it depends on you, be at peace with all men. Never take your own revenge, beloved, but leave room for the wrath of God, for it is written, "VENGEANCE IS MINE, I WILL REPAY," says the Lord. "BUT IF YOUR ENEMY IS HUNGRY, FEED HIM, AND IF HE IS THIRSTY, GIVE HIM A DRINK; FOR IN SO DOING YOU WILL HEAP BURNING COALS UPON HIS HEAD." Do not be overcome by evil, but overcome evil with good.

Philippians 1:27
Only conduct yourselves in a manner worthy of the gospel of Christ; so that whether I come and see you or remain absent, I may hear of you that you are standing firm in one spirit, with one mind striving together for the faith of the gospel.

Colossians 3:2
Set your mind on the things above, not on the things that are on earth.

Colossians 3:12-14
And so, as those who have been chosen of God, holy and beloved, put on a heart of compassion, kindness, humility, gentleness and patience; bearing with one another, and forgiving each other, whoever has a complaint against anyone; just as the Lord forgave you, so also should you. And beyond all these things put on love, which is the perfect bond of unity.

Titus 3:1-2
Remind them ... to malign no one, to be

uncontentious, gentle, showing every consideration for all men.

James 5:9
Do not complain, brethren, against one another, that you yourselves may not be judged; behold, the Judge is standing right at the door.

4
"Loaves and Fishes"

Cornerstone is made up of former Presbyterians, Baptists, Methodists, Catholics, Episcopalians, Lutherans, Pentecostals of every stripe, Disciples of Christ, Independents, and some I would be embarrassed to mention. We have rich and poor, blue collar and white, educated and uneducated, forty-year-old hippies, and a couple of cowboys. The three-piece suit in the communion line might be followed by ragged, faded blue jeans and worn-out tennis shoes. We have no homogeneous grouping. We are not even geographically close to one another. Many drive thirty to forty-five minutes to get to church.

This means there have been many different visions for Cornerstone. The first one, the one God gave and confirmed by outside prophecy, was that we would be a renewal church of the sort that folks would come to from far off in order to see and participate in what God was doing. This would be so not only in our own denomination, but also in the wider body of Christ. We also knew that we were called to be the sending church for Elijah House,

Birthing the Church

and so a significant part of our ministry would lie in healing families and restoring the inner man. We knew we were not called to be a small church. Small churches seem to have little impact on a national scale.

Early on, however, we absorbed a large number of folks whose vision of themselves was small, poor, and bound to stay that way. That vision of themselves was aggressively projected onto the church. For example: In July 1981 we were blessed to purchase 10 acres of land with a two-bedroom ranch-style house and a 1,700-square-foot barn. We had only been a church for 11 months and could in no way afford a land payment in addition to rent for the facility we had occupied up until then. So the house became the Sunday school building and the barn was cleaned up for use as a sanctuary. We laid a carpet of cedar shavings from a local shake mill and proceded to make the cheapest conversion we could manage so that we would be warm in winter. It had a certain charm, but it became the symbol of our infancy, our poverty, and our smallness. When we began to talk of future building plans in a responsible way, our "poor" raised a stink.

There is a difference between the poor and the financially embarrassed. The financially embarrassed individual has a positive self-image. He knows himself to be of real significance and value no matter what his situation is financially. One who is "poor" believes in his heart of hearts that he is small and *in*significant. Usually he can't admit this to himself and so he goes about associating with those who won't threaten his thin veneer of self-importance with their own success or confidence. He chooses and creates situations which are small enough that he can avoid facing his fear of insignificance. This is why our "poor" fought so hard to keep us small and accused me so vehemently of arrogance and ambition whenever I began to speak about growing and building.

I remember those months as times when our congregation had great difficulty attracting and holding "winners." One of our "poor" said to one of our "winners," "We don't need you here, rich man!" That rich man's real estate business was teetering on the brink of bankruptcy due to economic recession and some disastrous business reverses. He was, nevertheless, a man who had achieved something and who believed that God wants to bless His children both materially and spiritually. Our "poor" were deeply threatened by him. They were determined we would remain a "poor" church, reflecting in membership, program and facility our human situations and limitations. In their insecurity, growth would present the danger of diminished personal importance. I believe it kept us small longer than God really intended, and it certainly crushed the spirit of the church.

We still have many financially embarrassed members. As I write this chapter, the local unemployment rate is something like 25 percent. But our "poor" have left, and those who have not are repenting and learning to think like King's kids.

I have come to believe that every ministry has a specific vision or calling from God and that it must stick to that vision until God gives clear and powerful guidance to change. I have watched many national ministries, for instance, continually widen their activities until the original mission is smothered. What is left too often seems to be a marketing machine for the gospel product,

Birthing the Church

all flash and no real heart. I deeply respect evangelist Billy Graham because he has never been anything but evangelist Billy Graham. He has most profoundly impacted our nation because he has held to his original course without faltering, neither adding to nor taking away from the original vision. So we began to recover power and momentum as we returned to our original vision, still a heterogenous body divided by heritage, position, income, education and geography, but united by a common hope, and together rich in Christ. All things are possible with God. We began to design a program and a facility reflective of God's glory rather than our human limitation, and we had fun doing it. Ultimately the safeguarding of the vision is a hedge against disunity and is part of the glue which holds the family together. Paul said to Timothy (1 Tim. 4:14-15), "Do not neglect the spiritual gift within you, which was bestowed upon you through prophetic utterance with the laying on of hands by the presbytery. Take pains with these things; be absorbed in them, so that your progress may be evident to all." Stand by the calling and pursue it.

In Matthew 14 is the story of one of Jesus' miraculous feedings of thousands. The scene opens as John the Baptist has just been beheaded. Jesus had to be deeply hurt since John was the one who baptized Him and was the first to recognize Him for who He was. With a heavy heart he sought solitude for rest and, I think, to grapple in His heart with the cross which was to come. John's death had to have brought it a bit nearer. Galilee measures about 50 miles by 25 miles and, according to one contemporary historian, there were 204 towns and villages, none of which had a population of less

"Loaves and Fishes"

than 1,500. Where could He go for solitude in such a densely populated land?

On the far side of the Sea of Galilee was a place of wilderness, and since the lake was only eight miles across at its widest point, it was there Jesus sought to go via a fishing boat. But the multitudes saw and, guessing his destination, they scurried around the lake to meet Him. Because of their great haste, they were apparently not provisioned for the wilderness. Jesus graciously taught and healed through a long day without rest. Enthralled, none of the people thought to head for home and food until it was too late to do so and the crowd became hungry.

Reading the story I can feel the disciples thinking, "When do we get to rest?" The people's need for food seemed like a good excuse to be rid of them, but in the midst of their desperate fatigue, Jesus, wholly in character, blithely asked for the impossible. He said, "You feed them, all 5,000!" They complained that there were only five loaves and two fishes. Then our Lord made one of the simplest, most profound statements of His ministry. He said, "Bring them to Me." He blessed the food, probably by saying the ancient Jewish blessing, "Blessed art Thou, O Lord our God, King of the universe, who brings forth bread from the earth." The disciples then distributed five loaves and two fishes to 5,000 people. After everyone in that multitude had eaten his or her fill, each disciple gathered up one large basket of left-overs.

Parables are stories taken from the stuff of everyday life to illustrate and teach a point. An *acted* parable is one that is walked through and seen. It is a lesson lived, something experienced that points beyond itself. I believe this whole episode to be an acted parable in which a group of exhausted, overwhelmed disciples could participate and so learn some deep lessons. I believe those lessons involved giving when they didn't feel they had anything to give. The feeding of the 5,000 was a faith-stretcher designed to illustrate something concerning enormous giving from miniscule resources. For us at Cornerstone, it underscored the importance of getting past the "poor" man's attitude.

Lesson 1. *Jesus will not be put off by the smallness of our resources or by the size of the task.* He was continually admonishing His disciples to believe bigger, reach higher, think larger. "O men of little faith," He used to say. With faith like a mustard seed, a mountain could be moved (Matt. 17:20). According to Acts 1 the disciples were commanded to think in terms of witness to the ends of the earth. This He said to Galilean fishermen and country bumpkins. He also said of him who would believe: "The works that I do shall he do also; and greater works than these . . ." (John 14:12).

In the movie, *The Empire Strikes Back*, Luke Skywalker was levitating objects by using "the Force" under the guidance of his mentor, Yoda. Suddenly, Luke's spaceship sank into the swamp. Yoda commanded him to levitate it out, but Luke failed and exclaimed in defeat, "It's too big!" meaning that it was much larger than the small objects he had been levitating a few moments before. Yoda's response was wonderful, "No! not bigger! Bigger only in your mind! Judge you me by my size? . . ." In a beautiful monologue which could in many respects have come from the pages of Scripture, he

"Loaves and Fishes"

declared, "My ally is the Force, and a powerful ally it is." Therefore, his small size was not a consideration. Stretching forth his arms and concentrating, he then raised the ship from the water with considerable dispatch. "I can do all things through Christ who strengthens me" (Phil. 4:13).

Lesson 2. *In order for it to be enough, they had to bring the food to Jesus.* He said that He is the vine and we are the branches, that apart from Him, we can do nothing (John 15). Too often I have heard believers say to me, "I just can't. I'm not strong enough," or "You don't understand. It's too hard to forgive." People have told me they just could not speak in front of people or that a counseling situation was simply too big for them to handle. Most crippling of all to the church is the attitude that we are too small to be dreaming big dreams, in spite of Jesus' summons to bring what little we have to Him so that He can cause it to be enough and more.

Lesson 3. *Jesus does not demand from us wonders and plenitudes we do not possess.* He calls upon us simply to invest what we do have, small as it is. The parable of the talents (Matt. 25:14) makes just that point. Three men were given five, two and one talents respectively. Those having the five and two went out and invested. Fruit came and the master gave reward. Because of fear, the last man invested nothing. The master was angry. We don't have to be perfect, but we do have to make the investment of whatever resources are entrusted to our care. Then God is responsible for bringing increase. Our fear often tells us that our meager resources cannot possibly be enough to meet the need. That's the thinking of the natural man, but in Christ we have become

Birthing the Church

supernatural! The disciples were right. They didn't have enough to feed 5,000, but they did have Jesus.

When Cornerstone opened, we committed to ask for no denominational subsidy. Our local economy was crumbling. I had a family to feed. But the strength of God's calling moved us and we brought it to Jesus for blessing. Our first year's receipts ran in excess of $40,000. God didn't ask us for $40,000, but He did ask that we invest ourselves, our tithes, and our energies in an impossible task. The fruit would be His, so we invested and He gave the growth.

Lesson 4. *When the disciples had obeyed and invested their little in the overwhelming task, they had more left over than they began with.* The rule seems to be that the more of our minuscule resources we invest, the more we get in return. "Then Peter answered and said to Him, 'Behold, we have left everything and followed You; what then will there be for us?' And Jesus said to them, 'Truly I say to you, that you who have followed Me, in the regeneration when the Son of Man will sit on His glorious throne, you also shall sit upon twelve thrones, judging the twelve tribes of Israel. And everyone who has left houses or brothers or sisters or father or mother or children or farms for My name's sake, shall receive many times as much, and shall inherit eternal life' " (Matt. 19:27-29). Luke has it a little differently saying that we shall, "receive many times as much *at this time* and in the age to come, eternal life" (Luke 18:30). This is the law!

Our "poor" were afraid that if we grew or expanded our ministry beyond Post Falls, we would somehow lose our sense of intimacy. They were fearful, as well, that they would lose control. Those who moved on with us

"Loaves and Fishes"

came to understand what I learned growing up in a family of six children. Each time a child was born we had not less love, but more. That child was a gift, not a burden. He or she brought something and added it to us. When Beth and I had our third child, the love our family shared increased not 25 percent but really more like 100 percent! This is true as the body of Christ grows, *if* we choose not to hoard what God has given us, whether in love, in comfort, in spiritual resources, or in material goods.

When our "poor" were with us, we found that people actually felt pushed away and could not explain why. When the "poor" were gone, love grew and multiplied and so did our numbers. Within weeks of their departure, God blessed us with the gift of badly needed pews from another church. A sister church in California gave money for our altar. Elijah House and Cornerstone drew up an agreement whereby Cornerstone's tape ministry would do Elijah House's duplication. It was an account which initially produced 2,000 cassettes per month and grew from there. We were able to put an unemployed member to work and begin a credible building fund as well. We gave our little to God without reservation, without being bound by fear of the enormity of the task and vision. God did indeed bless!

Our numerical growth resumed in earnest in March and April of 1982. Let no one assume that we weren't frightened. What remained of our leadership core was bloodied, emotionally exhausted and wanting rather to retreat from the work for a while than shoulder anything new. In fact, for a time, one of the strange phenomena of our fellowship was that if more than half of our

Birthing the Church

leadership core were having emotional crises and staying home on a given Sunday, that would be the Sunday when the sanctuary would be packed with new people. It was unnerving to say the least.

In the midst of that exhaustion God renewed our vision for growth with faith-stretching projections for numbers of people to be added within even more faith-stretching periods of time. One night when the elders and wives met for prayer we asked the Holy Spirit how much growth to pray for in a six-month period. The number given was so astounding we sat numb in silent disbelief for a while. We spent the rest of the evening talking about fear and about Christ's Lordship over the Church. Our fear came from exhaustion. It made us forget that twelve tired disciples fed 5,000 by simply bringing what they had to Jesus. *He* is the Shepherd of the sheep. *He* would give the growth (Acts 2:47). *He* would take care of feeding the flock.

In that period of time I was often fearful that leadership could not be developed quickly enough, that a building could not be financed and built in time to house all who would come, that we would not have the resources to call and pay for an associate pastor. In every instance, His response to me was the same. "I am the Shepherd of the sheep. I will feed My flock." I am convinced that the secret of growth for the church universal is the heart-level conviction that Jesus is indeed Lord and Master, Shepherd of His flock. Cornerstone is not my church and I am not its provider. I am caretaker over that which is not my own. The owner of the sheep will never leave me unequipped to feed His flock.

5
A Theology for Unity

I am a preacher's kid, and while my memories of my father are tremendous, my recollections of the church are more like horrendous. I don't remember churches as being havens of love in any sense of the word. There was always a small group gathered about my folks who were moving in renewal and so had grasped the meaning of the Lordship of Jesus with its implications for love and peace, but the larger church rarely seemed to get the idea. My parents had asked the Lord to send them to troubled churches and He had obliged. Always when renewal in the Spirit came, there was war as new blood came pouring in and old blood dug in its heels in a fight to preserve its power. False accusations and rumors circulated in the community. Folks got angry. Votes were taken to determine whether to terminate the pastor. Jesus was crucified anew.

I remember that we never had any money because God was always fourth in line of priority for parishioners after business, family support and fun. Some who were leaders in the church spent more on smoking and on

Birthing the Church

feeding the dog than on the Kingdom of God. So I was always the kid with the floppy soles on his Buster Browns and holes in his socks.

I remember my father being severely reprimanded for instructing teenagers in the precepts of biblical sexuality, as if they were not already getting an education of another sort. I remember smoldering grudges, deadly worship (though the prayer groups were something else), meaningless Sunday School, and people satisfied with nothing. I grew deeply bitter with the church. It was God's church, not man's, and we had taken it from Him. It was not a haven, not afire with His love, and certainly not a place of unity.

Much of my childhood was lived in the 1950's. They seemed to me to be comfortable, secure years for the church in America, provided you didn't do anything nonconformist as my parents did. The really critical years for me, however, were lived in the 1960's (I am high school class of '69), which were, by contrast, a decade when every mainline denomination in the country, including our own, was losing hundreds of thousands of members. It was also a time of great ecumenical discussions, when the World Council of Churches, the National Council of Churches and the Consultation on Church Union were making headlines. It was a time when another movement, which truly cut across denominational lines and really seemed to accomplish unity among its participants (at least at first) was being accused of divisiveness by mainline denominational Christianity. Enter the charismatic movement. My parents were part of it and it was on account of it that some of the heaviest fire came.

A Theology for Unity

As a result of all this ferment, both at home and in the wider church, it seems I was practically born with two questions in my heart. What makes a church grow, and what is the basis of true unity? Since this is not a book about church growth (others have done that work well enough), I'll tackle the unity question. I want to do that by means of a simple, personalized, theological statement taken from the prayer of Jesus for His disciples (John 17) just before His crucifixion.

The crux of the unity issue is addressed in John 17:15-26. Our Lord had two requests. First, He wanted the disciples sanctified. The word is *hagiazein* in the Greek, which means "to be made holy." That which is holy is that which is set aside for divine use. To be made holy is, therefore, to be set aside for God's task. It is to become somehow different from others because of that task. For the disciples the prayer is that they will be set aside to serve Him in and because of the Word of God. Jesus is saying, "I'm leaving. Set these aside to carry on in My Word."

His second request was for a unity that would make effective their ministry of and in that Word. John 17:21 gives us a vision of unity reflective of the Trinity, the central doctrine of all truly Christian faith. Trinity is our word for a wonderful, impossible, miraculous mystery, one God in three persons, yet not three Gods. It is a contradiction not rationally comprehensible or reconcilable. Only spiritually can it be perceived and understood by those graced of God to experience it. That model of perfected, impossible, mysterious oneness breaking in upon a people who are called to be God's own leads a world to believe that God sent Jesus Christ, "That they

Birthing the Church

may all be one; even as Thou, Father, art in Me, and I in Thee, that they also may be in Us; that the world may believe . . ." (John 17:21). How the world loves a mystery! As Jesus is one with the Father, so are we in the body of Christ with one another, for, "so we, who are many, are one body in Christ, and individually *members of one another*" (Rom. 12:5). "Now you *are* Christ's body, and individually members of it" (1 Cor. 12:27). "There is one body and one Spirit, just as also you were called in one hope of your calling, one Lord, one faith, one baptism, one God and Father of all who is over all and through all and in all" (Eph. 4:4-6).

That unity *is* the witness because it is so unique that it can't be explained. It can only be spiritually understood and experienced. Our witness is neither doctrine, nor personal testimony, nor door knocking, nor preaching, nor teaching, but that incomprehensible, impossible bond of love, the way in which the church moves and breathes as one while each individual becomes not less himself but more uniquely special. That is the Trinitarian stamp. When it is present and on display, the world says, "I don't understand it, but I see it, and I want it."

I have found that such togetherness comes not from striving for it by focusing on the oneness or on one another, but from a corporate and individual effort to be one with Jesus. All the rest is byproduct. My spine tingles at the thought of what might occur if Christians ever learned, as Jesus did, to do only what they saw their Father doing.

Disunity is the result of wrong focus. It comes when we forget that we are not in this to be self-serving but

A Theology for Unity

Christ-serving. It comes when we forget that it is His church, not ours, His project, not ours, and for His glory, not ours. We are off base when we begin to use the church as a means to bolster our sense of self-importance. We rend the fabric of our union when we begin to speak about who's going to "win" an argument. Worst of all, we insure disunity by filling up our vision with the effort to love one another until we end up in an idolatry of loving one another. Idolatry *always* leads to disunity.

If we begin by striving for corporate and individual union with the Lord Jesus Christ in the person of His Spirit, our oneness as a church will follow, stamped with the mystery of the Trinity as we are members of one another. "And the glory which Thou hast given Me I have given to them; that they may be one, just as we are one; I in them, and Thou in Me, that they may be perfected in unity, that the world may know that Thou didst send Me, and didst love them, even as Thou didst love Me" (John 17:22-23). His glory was His oneness with His Father. That glory granted to us results in the attractive mystery of loving unity. Let us therefore pursue that glory, "... that the love wherewith Thou didst love Me may be in them, and I in them" (John 17:26).

6
Worship

Obviously, worship is the central act of the church. The world can duplicate any other activity in which we engage, but only the church can truly worship. All our activities must be energized with the awe and power of the worship experience. In relation to this experience I have both grief and joy.

The grief is that the church universal seems largely to have lost its worship sense. I speak as one who grew up in mainline denominational Protestantism and I know that in the average local congregation less creative attention has been paid to worship than to almost any other activity. This is a particular passion for me since it was the worship experience which I believe carried our moody, strife-ridden congregation through the first year. Without it we most certainly would not have survived. The joy is that I see God moving to restore the worship of the church and I see this as one of the primary callings for those of us who call ourselves "charismatic."

The typical mainline denominational worship service includes five to ten minutes for announcements, another

Birthing the Church

five to ten minutes for an offering, perhaps one to three minutes for a greeting and a handshake (if it's a friendly congregation), and twenty or thirty minutes for a sermon. It all adds up to forty or fifty minutes of newsreel, giving, fellowship, and proclamation. That's forty to fifty minutes of the precious hour set aside each week for worship spent on nonworship items. It does include three to five minutes in a pastoral prayer or a silent people's prayer and ten to twelve minutes on the traditional three or four hymns. That's only ten to fifteen minutes of the worship hour spent in activity which could in any true sense be identified with worship. Then, to add insult to injury, the hymns are usually done in such a perfunctory manner as to evidence little difference between congregational singing and instrumental solo.

The result is that the average parishioner attends church not because of the worship but because the people are nice, or the sermons are good, or because the congregation has good Bible studies, or simply from long habit and duty. These all are good reasons, but none of them are most important.

From puberty onward I have been a showman with a sixth sense for where "the people" are and for the sorts of forces that compete for their attention. I spent my high school years tramping the Pacific Northwest with a rock group I led and promoted. I am not advocating that atmosphere as healthful for anyone's spiritual development, but it did teach me that our world is full of fun and exciting, worldly things to do, all of which are competing for the attention of our people. What we present in church, therefore, had better be more real, more meaningful and more exciting than the lure of the world.

Worship

As memberships have continued to shrink, the mainline denominations have commissioned studies to determine causes of their losses. Many have been named. As a showman, however, I know that one of the most significant single causes is that the church simply can't compete with the world. We can't compete because we have forgotten how to worship in the power of the Spirit and so have lost our ability to let God inspire awe.

Let's begin, therefore, with an understanding of worship. Worship begins with praise. Praise is simply the act of complimenting or acknowledging the goodness of a person or thing. Absalom was praised by Israel for being good-looking, even though he tried to take his father's kingdom by force. Joash was praised because he was a good king after his predecessor had been a bum. We praise athletes, beautiful women, wine, food, and so on. Praise, as the act of compliment, can be applied both to things and to God. Worship, by contrast, applies only to that which is divine and it occurs on an entirely different spiritual plane.

Praise is a human activity which acknowledges God. Worship is God's activity in us in response to praise as He catches us up to Himself in loving embrace. Worship is fraught with the wonder of an intimacy in which God has taken the initiative. In worship we move past what we are doing as human beings and we become lost in what He is doing in and through us. Praise prepares us, but no more than that.

It follows that praising God without persevering to a point of breakthrough into worship is like preparing a sumptuous Thanksgiving meal, smelling the turkey and pumpkin pie cooking all day, setting it out on the table, admiring it in mouth-watering fashion, only to go out to McDonald's and leave the food on the table. Even worse, some of us never so much as get the turkey thawed. We leave the dinner in the freezer and sit down at an empty table to read recipes and talk about what it might have been like.

Of the many Old Testament Hebrew words for "worship," *shachah* is a common one. It means "to bow the self down." God increases; I decrease. I am awed by Him. My self dies, and with it my honor, my dignity, my pride. In Exodus 34:5-9 Moses obtains a glimpse of God as He passes by on Mount Sinai, and immediately falls on his face. In Joshua 5:13-15, Joshua meets an angel of the Lord who has come to captain the Lord's host and he instantly prostrates himself. This is the meaning of *shachah*, to fall on one's face, overcome. In it there is little room for human dignity. God's dignity, yes! But human dignity, no!

Proskuneo appears frequently as the word for worship in the New Testament. It's primary meaning is "to bow down" or "to prostrate oneself," but one root meaning is something like "to kiss reverently." It was at one time used of the act of bowing down to kiss the "earth mother" when Greek sailors would return from a voyage and is, therefore, a term which can include intimacy as well as self-abnegation. Worship is an intimate love relationship with God in which I surrender all honor and initiative to Him.

Revelation 5:8-14 gives us a picture of heavenly worship. I believe we ought to pattern our worship after the heavenly prototype as much as possible. What we see in the passage is a repeated occurrence in the Book of

Worship

Revelation and demonstrates to us that true worship reaches our "tremble level." It plucks our deepest inner chords with the result that we are utterly undone. In Revelation 5:8 the worshipers are identified as the twenty-four elders and the four living creatures which, to make matters brief, seem to be the most powerful beings in the universe next to God. They begin with praise, which in Revelation 5:9 is a collective, poetic recital of what Jesus has accomplished for His people. They are then joined by an uncountable angel chorus attributing to Jesus a sevenfold blessing of the attributes of God (Rev. 5:12). The crescendo rises as all of creation joins loudly in attributing glory to Jesus, the Lamb (Rev. 5:13). The result is that the elders, "fell down and worshiped" (Rev. 5:14), overcome, the most powerful beings in the universe made glad to be without personal honor so that honor might be rendered.

I have come to believe that the most crucial element in worship is a surrender level attained solely by obedient pursuit of the act of praise to a point of divine breakthrough which overwhelms. Praise, by itself, is a powerful activity, but it can be done without real surrender. I can even use it to try to manipulate God by means of my faith in the power of praise. Worship in the truest sense is the step beyond and is therefore not consistently attainable by spiritual babes unwilling to die to self or unwilling to pursue the obedience of praise without regard for whether they "feel" like it or not. Like the twenty-four heavenly elders we need to be willing to surrender the guardianship of our honor and dignity to Him who is the author of all true honor and dignity.

Another way of looking at it is via the analogy of a love

affair in which the partners continually compliment each other. Each compliment releases energy into the relationship until they no longer have power in the relationship, but the power of the relationship has them. Yet another perspective is that of an orchestra or choir in which each musician practices diligently, both independently and as part of the group, until in the concert every member plays his heart out with the result that something somehow greater than the sum of all the parts is created and all are awe-stricken. Praise is the human activity of rehearsal. Worship is the divine activity in concert which makes us more than the sum of our individual selves. We are caught up and carried by the "music."

In praise, we minister to Him. In worship, He ministers to us. But we must pursue that discipline of praise as we would a rehearsal for a choir concert until He breaks in upon us to carry us away. In that sense our worship is not our own, but rather His gracious act in the Holy Spirit in us.

In our early days, amid all the trouble, we were a terribly moody congregation. Sometimes I think we still are, but especially in the beginning I never knew what would walk through the door on a Sunday morning. One week we would blow the roof off with the power of our song, and the next week my guitar alone could drown out an entire congregation. Several things saved us.

First, and most importantly, was the grace of God who is the head of the church. He is faithful to inspire and to move His people if we give Him but the barest of invitations. Second, I knew clearly what sort of style God wanted to develop at Cornerstone. This is crucial for any

Worship

pastor or worship leader. We can't just blindly grope and expect to arrive. Within the bounds of each tradition, whether liturgical or nonliturgical, high church, or low church, we must creatively lead our people into a corporate expression—appropriate to them—of the biblically mandated balance that consists of order, discipline, spontaneity and congregational participation as revealed for us in 1 Corinthians 14 and Ephesians 5:18-19 (to name just two passages). Let not the people perish for lack of a vision. We who lead must know what we want, in the Lord, to see our people doing in the worship experience. That vision can take as many forms as there are Christian traditions. Within each tradition, practice, or liturgy is room for true "charismatic" or Spirit-inspired and Spirit-gifted worship on the biblical pattern of order, discipline, spontaneity and congregational participation in balance. Each leader must find, on his knees, the appropriate, creative mix and style which God has planned for each individual congregation.

That leads me to the third thing which saved us in our worship that first year and a half. I am a counseling pastor. I teach counseling at professional and lay seminars all across the country. God led me to use that gift in my worship leadership of our emotionally unstable, moody congregation. I became, Sunday after Sunday, a corporate counselor to a collective entity in order to lead the people to a genuine encounter with God. He who would lead, I discovered, must work on sharpening his gift of discernment to know where the people are so that he can begin to coach, plead, instruct, and even rebuke them toward the goal of worship for their good. I could feel the hearts of the people in my heart. I could see them spiritually. Often, on the basis of my perceptions, I would stop the progress of the service to ask questions like, "How many are afraid today? Why?" or, "How many have become really discouraged this week? Why?" Such questions could then be followed by a brief word of instruction about how to rise above the mood to enter into worship and so be fed. Often my response was a rebuke, sometimes gentle and sometimes not so gentle. I might call for public confession of sin together with repentance. I might ask for praise to be voiced which would express and affirm the nature of God in relation to our human fears and hurts. I might call for Scripture to be read which would apply to the problem. We might call for some sort of "devotion in motion" to break them loose. My job was to move them from where they were to where God wanted them to be. That's what a shepherd does with his sheep.

The ultimate goal is to reach maturity which, according to Ephesians 4:14-16, means a depth of unity based on Christ-likeness, leading to stability, dependent on the proper functioning of each member of the body as each member holds fast to the head who is Christ. That's when the leader does not really lead, but rather the Holy Spirit freely carries all of us together in peace. Until that time the leader is equipping and enabling the people as a corporate counselor of a collective entity.

At no time does the leader have the right to succumb to the mood of the people if that mood is not edifying or glorifying to Christ. Neither does the leader have the right to succumb to his own mood. During the worship hour I will be what the sheep need me to be for their edification and, at the same time, I will worship in my

Worship

own heart as if no one else were present. I will minister to the people where they are in order to lift them, but I will not allow my joy to be stolen by anyone else's disobedience or depression. That wasn't easy to do in the midst of crisis and there were many times when I failed, but always, every Sunday, God made His breakthrough and rescued us all so that we survived our hard times. I persevered because I knew that, if I did not model it for the people, they would never get the idea. The rule is, "What you want the people to be doing, do for them at first and in front of them. In the end they will follow."

Briefly, our style at Cornerstone is to begin with forty-five minutes or so of contemporary worship songs and choruses interspersed with spontaneous praise, prophecy, tongues and interpretation, or any other edifying activity the Spirit might deem appropriate to the moment and edifying to the group and/or individuals. All praise and prayer aloud is rendered one person at a time, so that all are edified. Some among us came out of classical Pentecostal traditions and were grateful not to have to try to worship through the cacophony of a whole congregation shouting individual praises all at once. On the other hand, we lost a number of Pentecostals precisely because we did not make all that noise. God makes room for different styles and traditions to meet different needs.

When I, or the worship leader, sense that we have made the worship "connection," we are free to move on to the message which usually lasts thirty minutes, more or less. The message is followed by a very liturgical Eucharist in which I try to use both ancient and scriptural sources for responsive readings and singing.

Birthing the Church

My favorite source is the Episcopal *Book of Common Prayer*, although we are a United Church of Christ. We use a common cup, providing both grape juice and real kosher wine, together with real matzohs (or a close facsimile thereof) for unleavened bread. The congregation comes forward to receive while spontaneous congregational singing is carried on in the background.

In broad outline, that is our style. All the components of it can be incorporated into any tradition to the degree and in the balance appropriate to each locale. The important thing is to meet the living God in such a way that worship in Spirit and in truth is accomplished. the result is that God carries us. That can happen whether your praise is liturgical or spontaneous or somewhere in between.

7
The Corporate Body

I, therefore, the prisoner of the Lord entreat you to walk in a manner worthy of the calling with which you have been called, with all humility and gentleness, with patience, showing forbearance to one another in love, being diligent to preserve the unity of the Spirit in the bond of peace. There is one body and one Spirit, just as also you were called in one hope of your calling; one Lord, one faith, one baptism, one God and Father of all who is over all and through all and in all (Eph. 4:1-6).

One of the most difficult lessons for any body of Christ to learn is the lesson of corporateness. From the moment that one becomes a Christian, nothing he does or experiences will ever again be entirely private. From that moment forth, his fortunes are intertwined with those of all other believers. He has become a part of an organism to which he must be faithfully committed lest he die as a believer and become unfruitful. The nation of

Israel was one family, children of one father, Abraham. In Christ, by adoption, or by grafting in, every Christian has likewise become a son of Abraham with one God, one life. Henceforth we are a body such that, "... if one member suffers, all the members suffer with it; if one member is honored, all the members rejoice with it" (1 Cor. 12:26). My sin, no matter how private, defiles and hinders the progress of the whole church. My righteousness, no matter how private, releases blessing into the whole fellowship. I *need* the church. The church *needs* me.

This is a difficult concept for us westerners to absorb and understand. Our comprehension of it at Cornerstone runs in cycles, and I find myself preaching on it over and over again. This is so for several reasons. First, the tradition in our society is one of rugged individualism and self-centeredness. One carves his own clearing out of the wilderness with no help from you, thanks! Do your own thing. Fulfill yourself. Just me and God. My religion is private. I am not hurting anyone else with what I do! The biblical, Hebrew view is exactly the opposite. Deuteronomy 6 demands an openly public display of faith. Joshua 7 tells the story of Achan, who kept back some of the plunder of war which was to be destroyed. His individual, private act caused the whole nation of Israel to fail before its enemies because Achan had caused Israel to sin. I am individual, but I am also corporate by nature, and therefore responsible to and for others whose destinies are bound to mine by the Spirit of God.

The second reason we have such difficulty comprehending and acting on our corporateness is that too

The Corporate Body

many of us are children of divorce. While we were still small, a bomb was dropped on our sense of family and corporate oneness so that our grasp of permanence and of costly commitment got blown apart. It takes a decision and an act of will in faithful obedience to begin to rebuild it.

The third reason is that even when our parents stayed together, their parenting was of the absentee variety. What our parents modeled to us was, "Everything else first for my own fulfillment; family commitment last," and dead last is where the church as extended family comes in. When the schedule is crowded, it is the first to go because we have very little idea what it means to be self-sacrificially committed to other human beings who need us. Worse, too many of our parents weren't present to rejoice with us in our little victories and to weep with us over stubbed toes. They weren't there to make us stick with the hard job until it was done right. In a family I learn that if my sister is sick, my friends can't come in. If my brother gets a spanking and I laugh, I am next. If Dad is late for dinner, everybody waits. If Mom is mad at me today, an hour later she still loves me and she is still my Mom. We don't run from one another because we can't. We are family. That is the body of Christ.

The fourth reason can be described in terms of what Marshall McLuhan called hot and cold mediums. A cool medium is one which requires active participation by the one who receives it. A book is a cool medium because it's useless unless I activate it. Sheet music is a cool medium for the same reason. Hot mediums, by contrast, do it all for you. The problem is that our whole generation was raised on television, the epitome of the hot medium. Our

Birthing the Church

minds are geared to a passive mode, ready to be effortlessly entertained. Church is a cool medium. It requires our individual participation as a part of the corporate whole in order for it to work. The result has been a drop in overall church attendance. It's boring. In the 1970's the population of the United States grew by more than 10 percent, but the churches grew by only 4 percent. That means we're losing. For example: the United Presbyterian Church lost 16 percent. My own United Church of Christ lost 16 percent of its membership between 1973 and 1983, with my local conference dropping a whopping 33.2 percent as reported at the Annual Assembly of the Washington North Idaho Conference, June 4, 1983. The Mormons, by contrast, gained 25 percent, but they emphasize and demand participation and they foster the sense of corporateness.

The non-cult, truly Christian denominations are losing not primarily because of the rush toward liberal and humanistic theology (though this is a large part of the problem), but because we have not clearly addressed the problem of the church as a cool medium in a mentally lazy society. If we don't learn the depth of what I will now call "active corporateness," we are lost.

According to the Greek of Ephesians 4:11, the leaders in the church are themselves gifts to the body whose task it is (according to Verse 12) to train the *people* to do the work. The leaders are only coaches. When I was in junior high, we had a losing football team. About mid-season, a local policeman, Officer Runyon (Ossifer Onion to us), joined the coaching staff and began to make our lives miserable. Any lineman who didn't hit hard at the snap of the ball was likely to be thrown bodily into the fray by an angry Ossifer Onion. When practice closed with the running of laps, tail draggers were likely to feel the bite of Onion's cleats on the hind side. He made us work! And we hated him for it . . . until we won our next game and we carried him off the field on our shoulders. We knew who had won it for us.

My congregation knows that I will not let myself be satisfied by favorable comparisons of Cornerstone to other churches. I will only let up on us when we have played the best game God has called us uniquely to play. My delight is in seeing my *people* succeed. They would prefer to watch me play the game alone. ("You do it so well!") But if I allowed that, I would cripple the body. Therefore, I am a hard coach. I know how a running back feels when he runs as hard as he can only to be tackled because a couple of linemen missed their blocks.

The Greek root for "equipping" is *katartis*, which means consummate artistry. My job is to make consummate ministerial artists out of my people so that the body is built up. The root word for "built-up" is *oikodome*, and it refers to "household," a corporate word. The saints are trained to do the work and the result is a household.

Out of the household grows "the unity of the faith" (Eph. 4:13), which is based on the works we did together in pursuit of the great task. When I was playing in my rock group in high school, we found that after three years of hard work together we could make up songs on stage during a performance and play them perfectly because we could simply feel what each other was going to do. This kind of unity happened for me when I was in the world. It can happen for the church in the Kingdom as we struggle together for the faith of the gospel, resulting in a spiritual harvest of joy.

This unity results in the "knowledge of the son of God," which is the intimate, experiential, relational knowing of Jesus for which all of us so deeply long. Work done together results in unity which results in fellowship with Christ. Fellowship comes after unity because the most important lesson He wants us to learn is love in dedication to one another as we serve together.

Having then known Jesus, the fellowship becomes "a mature man." The word is *teleion*, and it indicates completeness. Nothing is left out. But maturity as a body (and by implication, individuals) is dependent on work done together which leads to unity, which leads to the experience of knowing Jesus.

Finally, then, we reach "the measure of the stature which belongs to the fullness of Christ." In other words, we play the best game He has designed for us to play.

Christians must understand that no significant growth can occur apart from work, leading to unity, resulting in the experience of Jesus, which brings us to maturity in reflecting His nature. We can't and won't be like Jesus apart from faithful participation in the corporate work. I will go a step further and say that such involvement needs to be focused in one local body, not scattered about to several churches and parachurch groups. Only in that unflagging commitment to a group of people who are sometimes unlovable can I develop the maturity to which Paul refers in Ephesians 4:14. "As a result, we are no longer to be children, tossed here and there by waves, and carried about by every wind of doctrine . . . ." At last, through faithful involvement in the corporate task, we come to emotional and doctrinal stability. I could

The Corporate Body

point to a half dozen who were emotional messes in our church but who are today reaching real stability because of a refusal to run away from the fellowship when the work became difficult or the heart fell apart. It also leads to a corporate stability. That moodiness I spoke of in the chapter on worship began to vanish when we began to understand and act on corporateness. In my counseling I have learned that no lasting healing is possible without this commitment.

Ephesians 4:16 is the summary statement—"from whom the whole body, being *fitted and held together by that which every joint supplies, according to the proper working of each individual part*, causes the growth of the body for the building up of itself in love." The key is "according to," that is, only as much as each one does his part. I sometimes tell my people not to complain to me that their lives are falling apart if they haven't made this commitment to corporate participation. The Book says we can't come to maturity and stability apart from it. The Book is right.

Finally, I tell them, "Don't bring your friends to church to meet the minister or to be ministered to. Bring them to meet the family. They have already met the minister, and he was you!"

8
The Problem of Home Fellowships

Acts 2:42 and following is a description of the program of the early church set in the context of the day of Pentecost when the Spirit fell in power on the whole body while the 120 were gathered in the upper room. They went pouring out into the street, full of the Holy Spirit, speaking in tongues so that Jews who had gathered from many nations for the holiday heard the gospel in their own languages and believed. Having thus been empowered by the Holy Spirit, they instinctively understood, and began to practice, some principles in their life together.

They understood from their backgrounds as Jews that when we come into Jesus Christ we become part of a body, a corporateness, and that becoming part of a body has certain implications which the people of Acts 2 lived out. I see the passage as a formula for spiritual success in the church. If we follow God's formula, then we'll be blessed. To the extent that we don't follow God's formula, we won't be blessed. The Word of God is absolute. The Word of God is law. We can't operate outside of the Word and expect to be fully anointed.

Birthing the Church

The passage reads, "They were continually devoting themselves . . . ." That is, all the time, without ceasing, they were focusing their whole consciousness, their whole thinking, eating, drinking, breathing, sleeping, and waking on the following elements: They were devoting themselves to the apostles' teaching, which for us means a dedication to learning the Scripture and to listening to the teaching of the Word of God. They were devoting themselves to fellowship, to being together as constantly as possible. They were devoting themselves to the breaking of bread. This does *not* mean they continually ate a lot; that would be ridiculous. It is a reference to the frequent celebration of the Lord's Supper. They were frequently availing themselves of the refreshment of the Lord's Body and Blood, proclaiming His death until He comes. They continually devoted themselves to prayer, which means that they were consumed with a desire and a heart for communication with God. No wonder Acts 2:43 reports that they kept feeling a sense of awe and that signs and wonders were taking place. Signs and wonders will occur when we obediently follow the biblical pattern.

"And all those who had believed were together, and had all things in common; and they began selling their property and possessions, and were sharing them with all, as anyone might have need" (Acts 2:44-45). When the Spirit of God moves on a people who are spending that kind of time together, it becomes very easy to share with one another because we not only come to love one another, but we are aware, firsthand, of one another's needs. Because no one gets lost in the wings, the body does not forget.

The Problem of Home Fellowships

The clearest statement of program begins in Acts 2:46. "And day by day continuing with one mind in the temple...." I deeply respect the early Christians. I hear too many believers saying, "When I go to church I don't get anything out of it," or "I don't get anything out of my home fellowship, so I don't go." We need to realize that the people who led the temple worship were the priests and that they were nearly pagan in many respects. They were collaborators with the Roman aggressors, and only a short time before this, they were the ones who saw to it that Jesus was crucified. Nevertheless, the believers continued with one mind in great unity, attending the temple service every day. The temple was the gathering place for the people of God. All of them came together from the various places to which they were scattered and all worshiped together as a larger body. In our local churches, the main Sunday service is our "temple" experience when all of us gather in one place to glorify God as an extended fellowship. It is the time of awe. The early Christians understood the power in that, that it was present even when the priests were dishonorable, so they didn't even wait for the Sabbath, but did it day by day!

"And breaking bread from house to house, they were taking their meals together with gladness and sincerity of heart...." I want to emphasize, beginning here, that the pattern of the early church was the house church. It seems that most of those house church meetings began with some first-century equivalent of potluck and the special sort of fellowship which occurs over food. Accordingly, our home fellowships at Cornerstone are encouraged to eat together often.

Birthing the Church

I believe the involvement of the individual in the life of the early church can be condensed to three basic elements. The first is the worship experience in the temple, the larger gathering of all the believers. The second is that time especially given to learning as they devoted themselves to the apostles' teaching. At Cornerstone, this equates with our adult education program which provides a variety of elective options ranging from the Second Coming of Christ to how to minister to alcoholics. Through our adult education courses, we seek to give concentrated, in-depth instruction in both the facts and skills of Christian life and ministry. Thirdly, they were meeting for fellowship in the homes of believers. Putting it in practical terms, each church must provide and encourage its members to be involved in a full program of worship, educational, and small-group experiences. A church that does so effectively will be "praising God, and having favor with all the people. And the Lord was adding to their number day by day those who were being saved" (Acts 2:47).

I will say without reservation or qualification that *every* believer needs to be involved in these three basic elements of church program on a regular and significant basis. I say boldly that any believer not regularly involved in that fullness, when that fullness is available, is walking in disobedience to God. Exceptions might be women whose husbands only allow Sunday attendance, or folks whose working hours conflict with meeting times, and the like, but I have little sympathy with other excuses. The believer who neglects any one of these three elements is not obeying Scripture, he is not obeying God, and to that degree God cannot bless him accordingly. I

The Problem of Home Fellowships

realize this sounds hard-nosed, but if we believe the Word of God, we'll believe it's true. If we don't believe this to be true, then we don't believe the Word of God.

Unmistakably, the house church is the biblical pattern. Acts 5:42 is set in the context of the apostles having been imprisoned and then released after being admonished not to teach. Instead of not teaching, they went every day to the temple and "from house to house proclaiming Jesus as the Christ." Why? Because the believers were meeting in houses to hear the Word of God. I envision scenes in one household with a dozen believers, and in another with twenty, and yet another with six in someone's living room, gathered for prayer and to hear the teaching of the apostles.

Acts 20:20 reports that Paul similarly taught both publicly and from *house to house* in Ephesus. Paul was a time-conscious individual. It was he who taught us to redeem the time because the days are evil (Eph. 5:16). He was most certainly not teaching one family at a time from house to house, but was instructing groups of believers, gathered in homes, six, eight, ten and twenty in a living room.

Romans 16:3-5 refers to the church which met in the house of Priscilla and Aquila even though the letter is addressed to the whole church in Rome. There was one church, meeting in many small groups in the homes of believers. The quirk in this passage is that apparently Priscilla was the leader of the church. In that culture, a woman was considered almost chattel, so it is interesting that she is mentioned at all. It is the home of Priscilla and Aquila, rather than just the home of Aquila. More than that, it was the custom to mention the leader first when

Birthing the Church

writing or speaking. Priscilla's name is recorded first; therefore she must have been the leader of that house church. Note also that Paul is careful to call any gathering of believers "the church." The implication is that, whenever and wherever any number of believers have gathered, the spiritual fullness of the church is present. Colossians 4:15 refers to another woman, Nympha, who apparently led a house church, since it met in her home. Again, there was a larger body of all the believers who were in Laodicea, but clearly it was divided into small groups meeting in homes. Philemon 2 refers again to a house church that met in the home of Philemon. The traditional American pattern of Sunday-only attendance and pastoral calling on individuals in homes would have been inconceivable to the early church. It is not scriptural, and it is not working anymore. By and large, the churches which pursue that pattern are not growing. The house church is scriptural.

Matthew 18:19-20 reads:

> Again I say to you, that if two of you agree on earth about anything that they may ask, it shall be done for them by My Father who is in heaven. For where two or three have gathered together in My name, there I am in their midst.

This is the importance of the house church. When we gather as a small group in the home, the fullness of the Holy Spirit is there, the fullness of the church is there, and the fullness of the power of God, even if there is no leader. I find I must again and again teach my congregation and remind them of this power present in the

The Problem of Home Fellowships

small gathering, lest we think it can only happen in the awe of the assembly.

1 Corinthians 14:26 teaches that when we assemble, each one should have a Psalm, a teaching, a revelation, a tongue or an interpretation—for edification. This is the ministry of the body of Christ. If this were intended to occur in the temple experience, how long would it take for several hundred believers to "each one" make a verbal contribution? It wouldn't and can't work. I don't see this as a reference to Sunday morning but to the working of the home fellowship where each one of a dozen believers *can* participate and develop the ministry gifts God has given. There it can work. In that setting each one can be a star in the Lord. Sunday morning is the time to come together and be awe-stricken and to be reminded again who our God is, but the home fellowship is where the individual develops his gifts of ministry, free to try new spiritual wings, and free to crash because the brothers and sisters will pick him up and dust him off.

James 5:16 says that we are to confess our sins to one another and pray for one another that we may be healed. How could that work in the temple experience Sunday morning? It would, again, take too long. It isn't intended for the assembly, but it can happen in a home fellowship. Who would stand before a hundred people and say that he committed adultery last night? Or that he cheated on his income tax? This is not intended to occur in the worship service, but in a home fellowship with six to twenty people who love and care and have time to listen. Those people understand you and have already committed to love you, so that they won't be taken aback by what you say. They will pronounce forgiveness over you in Jesus' name and pray for your healing. They will also keep their mouths shut about it later. Of course it's possible to be obedient to James 5:16 in one on one situations. I emphasize group settings, however, because of the wider edification to be achieved by group participation. The deepest and most lasting emotional healings of which I am aware came about in group settings. All learn from the vulnerability of one. The whole group profits from the way the leader or some skilled group member handles it and each member becomes a better ear for others and a more effective minister for the Lord. A healthy, non-defensive transparency often comes about for everyone and that can be a catalyst for the healing of many. The gift of trust fosters a greater depth of love among group members. Too often the easy availability of private confession becomes an excuse to flee from a needed public one. I still do lots of personal counseling and God blesses that ministry, but I often say, "Have you shared this with your home fellowship?"

Hebrews 10:23-25 reads:

> Let us hold fast the confession of our hope without wavering, for He who promised is faithful; and let us consider how to stimulate one another to love and good deeds, not forsaking our own assembling together, as is the habit of some, but encouraging one another; and all the more, as you see the day drawing near.

Let us spend some time thinking how we can stimulate one another to love and to good deeds. Let our thoughts

The Problem of Home Fellowships

be consumed with how we can maximize one another.

We are *commanded* of God (no option) not to forsake our assembling together. To the degree that we disobey the Lord, we are not blessed. How well can all of us encourage all the rest of us on Sunday morning? It would take too much time to do so personally. There are too many people. Where does it work the best? In the home fellowship where there are a dozen or so other people who have walked with you for several months or years and so understand you. They know where you are and can give you just the right word in the right way, because they are committed to love you.

Some believe that they contribute nothing because they never say anything. Most people have no idea what a ministry of presence their faces are, even if they never say a word. We don't always need to say words in order to be edifying to one another. When an individual shows up at a home fellowship, it says that he loves and cares about the people in the group. When he doesn't show, it says he doesn't care and it hurts. Maybe it shouldn't hurt, but it does. Not all believers are mature enough to handle the no-show, and so people are wounded and discouraged. The exhortation to encourage one another is for the home fellowship in a ministry of presence as well as of word. We know where one another are in our lives, and so we know what each one needs to hear.

Notice also the end-time urgency of Hebrews 10:25—"and all the more, as you see the day drawing near." This is the time of Christ's return in which our gathering in supportive home fellowships for mutual encouragement becomes crucial to survival. I believe the end time is fast approaching, and that God is moving ever more intensely on the church in relation to home fellowships for the development of gifts, for support and for encouragement. It is an increasingly urgent word. I believe that in the final analysis, the churches that do not hear this word may not survive as churches, or at least not as viable forces in the world.

If the believer is not part of a home fellowship, who knows when he is sick and can come to pray for him? When he finds himself in emotional trouble and in need of undergirding, where is the ready-made support system based on relationships already developed? In such a case he has two obstacles to overcome. He must establish a set of relationships in addition to overcoming the trouble he is in. If the relationship is already there, then not only is the group ready and in place to support when trouble strikes, but it can often see the trouble coming ahead of time and avert it. When people are involved in home fellowships, I hear very few complaints that needs aren't being met or that individuals aren't being cared for. I hear these complaints only from those who have removed themselves from the support system.

Without home fellowships, how do we nurture the baby Christians? Where will they find a place where it's safe to ask questions? Certainly not in the worship service. That would be disruptive. When one is young in the Lord, some of those questions can sound pretty stupid, so there needs to be a secure environment in which to unload and learn the basics of the faith from the lips and the experience of older saints. Where will they find a committed group to love them and care for them constantly? The nurture of babes occurs in families. That's what a house church is called to be. I say boldly that if any believer is not

The Problem of Home Fellowships

committed to and attending a home fellowship, then he is starving baby Christians and hindering the weak.

Without home fellowships the church is without structures for responding quickly and easily to needy situations. Suddenly a church member is unemployed. Now what does he do? Suddenly he is out of money and food. Where does he turn? If he is part of a home fellowship, they know about it almost before it happens and are there for support. Many times I have seen a home fellowship feed a needy member's family before the cupboards even got bare. We need that instant response to emergency situations.

Recently at Cornerstone I have noticed that there is an increasing number of emergencies I don't even hear about until they're over because the home fellowships responded so instantly. The church has an emergency loan fund, a clothes closet and a food closet, but I have noticed that those in home fellowships rarely use these resources because the home fellowships cover the need. Through decentralizing our in-house care of our own poor in this way, we have been able to offer more to the poor outside of our church. At the same time, the believers grow in love and holiness as they personally meet needs and make sacrifices for one another. I know, for instance, of a single working mother who wrote a $500 check to another single, unemployed mother to prevent her eviction from her home and to feed her children. It wasn't easy to do, but both of them grew. My wife and I took in an unemployed nurse who had been sleeping on the street. Our home fellowship clothed her (her belongings had been stolen) and eventually bought her the Bible she had been praying for. Now she's on her

Birthing the Church

feet and an active member of the church.

Without home fellowships we have no constant, close environment to develop the gifts of the Spirit. We are called to minister to one another, but without a home fellowship, where does an individual get the chance to practice regularly? Home fellowship provides a secure environment in which to stumble and fall as we begin to walk in the gifts—tongues, interpretation, prophecy, words of knowledge, prayer for healing, and so on. Home fellowship is a place where we have the right to fail and be dead wrong. In that setting the body of Christ is able to help us understand where we were—or are—off the beam and how to get back on. They are our check and balance. For instance, if a bad word is delivered in the spontaneous portion of the Sunday worship service, lots of people can get hurt. In the home fellowship, however, it can more easily be questioned, sorted and sifted. The speaker will be loved anyway, because he is known and because a personal commitment exists.

Perhaps the most important thing that's lost without the home fellowship is a setting in which to work out *agape* love. *Agape* is often described as unconditional love. I define it as a commitment to love you today when I feel like it and to love you tomorrow when I don't feel like it. I told you I would be there at seven o'clock Thursday night; I don't feel like it, but that is what I told you and so for your sake I'll be there. I have chosen to make your needs more important than my own. As I have observed the body of Christ at work, I have seen that until we get into home fellowships we have a much more difficult time coming to understand our responsibility, both to love when we feel like it and to love when we don't feel

The Problem of Home Fellowships

like it—"I will be there for your sake because you need me." Any believer who walks away from a home fellowship thinking that the group doesn't need him is dead wrong and is a liar to himself. If he brings no more than his presence together with that measure of the Holy Spirit which is his, then he will have made a contribution of inestimable value.

We need to hear the message of John 21:15 and following. It was after the Resurrection and Peter had left the ministry to return to fishing. Jesus said, "Simon, son of John, do you love me more than these?" And I think He pointed to the fish. Peter assured Him that he did. Jesus said to him, "Tend My lambs." Jesus asked him again and with a note of impatience Peter repeated his assurance. Jesus said again, "Shepherd My sheep." For a third time Jesus asked him, knowing that he hadn't yet grasped the point. Peter, with some real exasperation, said yes again, and Jesus responded, "Tend My sheep." I believe that on the third plea Peter heard at last. I have said to our people, "Don't tell me that you love Jesus if you haven't learned to tend the sheep." Tending the sheep is the primary business of the home fellowship, where every believer is a shepherd and a priest.

In my own home fellowship, which is the pastor's home fellowship, because we are leaders of the flock, we find ourselves as individuals burdened in the Spirit and not knowing where it came from. But we can come together on a Friday night and discover that all of us, hallelujah, had the same burden and didn't understand it. We can then sit down to pray and listen to God until He reveals the source of the problem. We find the burden is lifted from us all as we pray for the problem. Usually it involves the condition of the flock, so that after we have prayed for it the church lurches forward in the Spirit the following Sunday. Sometimes I come to the group hurting and unable to lift myself. I ask for help and the group begins to question and probe until there is an understanding of where I am. Then their insights and prayers with laying on of hands are brought into play to lift and to restore me. Others in the group get similar support. We aren't perfect, and sometimes someone who has a need gets passed over altogether and then we're angry, but the next meeting we're still brothers and sisters committed to be there for one another. We live it through together and we work it out in love because in Christ we can do no other. I can bring my decisions to that group, my joys, fears, hurts and doubts. In so doing, I obey our Lord in His command that we should ". . . be subject to one another in the fear of Christ" (Eph. 5:21). I have learned to respect their insights and, in most cases, to take their advice.

Home fellowships are the most difficult aspect of church life. Everywhere I go I hear the same cry from pastors concerning them. People don't want to be involved. They don't want to be involved because they have never known that Hebraic sense of corporateness which so infuses the Word of God. They don't know how to be one with one another. So home fellowships weren't and aren't an easy element of congregational life to maintain. I worked several months training an initial group so that it could divide and become several groups. All but one of the first four groups failed. I had begun with a model that required intensive daily Scripture study by each member of the group. When everyone was faithful in

The Problem of Home Fellowships

study it worked and when they were not, it floundered. People—even Christian people—are by nature not faithful. I'm convinced that any program of the church, for the whole church, that is predicated on the assumption that believers will be faithful will fail.

I went to work again and came up with a pattern that includes a time of worship in song, praise and prayer; a time of sharing and—if need be—confession and ministry, and a time of Scripture study. The time of Scripture study is led by the group leader, who uses a study guide written by me. In that way, I assure a rich study time which doesn't require a lay person to have knowledge he doesn't possess or to invest time he may not have. They are written in such a way that a conscientious leader can add his own insights, but it isn't absolutely necessary that he do so. I also set the study guide up as a series of questions designed to draw the group into a discovery of the truth for themselves as they examine facts, reveal attitudes and deal with obedience.

I have heard every objection in the book to being involved in a home fellowship. "I am not getting anything out of it," is countered by, "Then learn to put something into it. God called you to serve and that itself is the lesson." "I just can't get along with so and so," is countered by, "God didn't ask if you liked him. He just said to love and serve him and that itself is the lesson." Those of us who have worked with home fellowships can think of many more excuses, but none of them can be substantiated from the Word of God. We need to have the courage to say so plainly as pastors and leaders.

I had trouble for a time in instituting a covenant in our groups. I found that if a covenant is foundationally an

Birthing the Church

agreement we make with one another, then it becomes a legalism by which we beat one another to death. But if we see it as an agreement we make with God, on the basis of Scripture, in relation to one another, then we are accountable to God alone and can set one another free. People end up being more faithful under the second model than under the first. Covenant in Scripture seems to be an agreement between God and Israel which is the basis for God's blessing. When Israel honors the covenant, God blesses, and when the nation doesn't honor the covenant, judgment comes. The home fellowship covenants we ask our members to own are as follows:

Colossians 3:5-14
The Covenant of Grace. I will love you, upbuild you and accept you, my brothers and sisters, no matter what you say or do, what you don't say or don't do. I love you in whatever form you come.

Ephesians 4:25-32
The Covenant of Truth. I will not hide from you what I feel about you or coming from you, good or bad, but I will seek, in the timing of the Spirit, to deal openly and directly with you in a loving and forgiving way so that you are not unaffirmed when in need, and so that our frustrations with each other do not become bitterness.

Luke 11:37-41
The Covenant of Openness. I will open myself to you inwardly, my hurts, joys, loves, hates, hopes, disappointments, history. I will affirm

you by needing you and making you part of my inner life.

Philippians 2:1-11
The Covenant of Sacrifice and Prayer. Particularly in our gatherings, but through the week as well, I covenant to seek to make your needs more important than my own as we talk, worship and pray together. I will pray daily and diligently for you. I will work to be sensitive to the Spirit concerning you.

Acts 2:43-47
The Covenant of Availability. I will seek to serve you with my time, energy, wisdom, finances, material goods. When you need my physical aid, I will be present with anything I have.

Hebrews 10:19-25 and Luke 9:57-62
The Covenant of Regularity. I will regard the regular time which my group spends together weekly as time under the discipling hand of Jesus in our midst. I will not grieve the Spirit, or hinder His work in the lives of my brothers and sisters by my absence except in emergency. By His permission and through prayer alone will I consider absence.

Ezekiel 3:16-21 and Matthew 18:12-20
The Covenant of Accountability. I give you the right to question, confront and challenge me in love when I seem to be failing in any aspect of

my life under God, family, devotions, general spiritual growth, and the like. I trust you to be in the Spirit and led of Him when you do so. I need your correction and reproof so that I may ever better fulfill God-given ministry among you. I covenant not to be defensive. (See Proverbs 12:1, 15; 13:1, 10, 18, and others.)

Proverbs 10:19; 11:9, 13; 12:23; 13:3; 15:4; 18:6-8
The Covenant of Confidentiality. I realize that much of what we share would be harmful to you who shared it, were it repeated in other company. Therefore, personal matters stop here. I will say nothing outside the group that might be injurious or embarrassing to any one of you.

Matthew 25:31-46
The Covenant of Outreach. I covenant to find ways to sacrifice myself for those outside our fellowship or our faith in the same ways I have covenanted to sacrifice myself for you, my brothers and sisters. I will treat unbelievers exactly as if they were believers. I will do it in Jesus' name so that others are added to the Kingdom of God in His love.

Each group is responsible for the care of all the church members in its geographical area, whether or not all those in that area are regulars at the group meeting. Names are assigned to group members once a month so that telephone calls can be made. We simply ask what we

The Problem of Home Fellowships

can pray for in their lives or if there are any needs we can meet. In this manner the body of Christ is involved in pastoral care, and the groups are forced to turn outward in love. The general rule from the Word of God is that anything turned in upon itself and existing for its own sake is an idolatry and will fail. So, each group needs to develop an outside vision for ministry. That vision can be service-oriented toward hospital, rest home or prison visitations. It can be care oriented as it looks after the welfare of other church members. It can be evangelistically oriented as the group seeks to grow. Whatever the vision, each group needs that outward thrust in order to be healthy.

In group outreach and in group meetings, we are seeking to foster in each member the following ministries:

1. A ministry from the Word of God according to 1 Corinthians 14:26.
2. A ministry of prayer according to Ephesians 6:18.
3. A ministry of personal and material availability according to Acts 2:44.
4. A ministry of presence according to Hebrews 10:24-25.

Each church will need to work out the form of home fellowship for itself, but these elements all need to be present.

I would encourage pastors and leaders not to give up if they find the groups are difficult to maintain or even if groups fail. The temptation is to try easy programs and, if they don't work quickly, to discard them in favor of something else. We need to remember that we are not in business to generate cheap excitement but to nurture deeply disciplined discipleship. Therefore, we need to do what is right rather than what "works," and we need to do it *until* it works. We need to do it because God has commanded it.

I'll close with an illustration of the interdependence of the three elements of biblical program in their effect on the life of the church. We experienced a growth spurt in the late summer and fall of 1982. Some miraculous healings were occurring, and the power of the Spirit in worship was growing. The church had matured and stabilized, and the second set of home fellowships was about a year old. We also had expanded our adult education into an elective program for the first time with several options available, rather than just one, and attendance was excellent.

In mid-October attendance at both the home fellowships and adult education started a nose-dive. At first the effect on worship was negligable, but in early November I went on a speaking trip. While I was gone, the bottom fell out of the worship experience. The peoples' hearts were simply dead to receive. The week after I returned, it was the same. Attendance was still up at the worship service, but the power was gone. That week one home fellowship had so few in attendance that it couldn't meet. Too many had decided they would rather be entertained than actively serve the Lord. I delivered a sermonic cannon blast concerning home fellowships and adult education, and indicated that if we didn't hear the Word and act upon it, God would take our blessing and give it

The Problem of Home Fellowships

to another. We had been warned before. Home fellowships returned to normal, then grew, and the power of our worship returned immediately.

The backbone of the New Testament church is the home fellowship, but it takes a hard-nosed, determined coach to keep it afloat. When the coach does his job, the results in deepened maturity, ministry skills and spiritual power are well worth the pain and effort.

9
Family and Church: A Biblical Balance

One of our stated missions as a church is to work for the restoration of the Christian family as expressed in the home and in the body of Christ. The simple principle is that the body of Christ is an extention of the family that lives with me in my home. All of us at Cornerstone agreed on that one. But some confusion entered on the question of how we ought to work out priorities. I had always accepted the teaching that our priorities should be "God first, family second, church third, and world last," but I was vaguely aware that I really couldn't live with it. I began to see that our leaders in Cornerstone were more torn apart by it than edified. It hurt the ministry and ultimately did *not* strengthen families as far as I could see. On that basis, I concluded that our assumption was amiss and that we had not understood what the Word of God has to say on the matter.

I found that the Word gives careful instruction concerning how to love and discipline children, at what age to carry out discipline and what age to let a child go, the power of blessings and cursings from a parent to a child, how and what to teach children, how to relate to parents after marriage, how to make love, how to live with a mate, headship and authority in the home, divorce, and what to do when a mate is an unbeliever. It is clear from God's Word that the family is the crucible in which people are formed. It is, indeed, central to God's plan for us. The union of one man and one woman in marriage is the cornerstone of human creation in God's image (Gen. 1:26-27). *Adham* (mankind) in the fullest sense comes really from the fullness of the union of *Ish* (*the* man) and *Isha* (woman). Family is therefore the base of operations for each individual. According to Scripture, if I don't handle my family well, I am not to be trusted to handle the church well in a leadership position (1 Tim. 3:4-5).

So Scripture has given a magnificent set of guidelines for the family and has exalted family to a role of foundational importance for the development of human beings. What it has clearly *not* given us is a cast-in-iron formula for balancing family commitment with church commitment. More clearly, it has certainly *not* said that family comes first. Such a teaching can't even be validly condensed from the *spirit* of the Word. In fact, I can't find a single instance of a scriptural personality experiencing a tension between commitment to family at home and commitment to God's people at large, except in 1 Corinthians 7 where Paul warns of that possibility under special conditions of persecution. In fact, the biblical warning is that family must never become an end in itself.

Matthew 10:34-37 reads:

Family and Church: A Biblical Balance

> Do not think that I came to bring peace on the earth; I did not come to bring peace, but a sword. For I come to SET A MAN AGAINST HIS FATHER, AND A DAUGHTER AGAINST HER MOTHER, AND A DAUGHTER-IN-LAW AGAINST HER MOTHER-IN-LAW: AND A MAN'S ENEMIES WILL BE THE MEMBERS OF HIS OWN HOUSEHOLD. He who loves father or mother more than Me is not worthy of Me; and he who loves son or daughter more than Me is not worthy of Me.

The statement is not made in the context of attitudinal priorities as we are often taught, but of priorities of ministries in the bearing of the cross (verse 38). In Luke 14:26-27 the same sort of statement is made, again with reference to the pursuit of the ministry of the cross:

> If anyone comes to Me, and does not hate his own father and mother and wife and children and brothers and sisters, yes, and even his own life, he can not be My disciple. Whoever does not carry his own cross and come after Me cannot be My disciple.

A young man came to Jesus (Matt. 10:21 and following) asking to follow Him, but to be allowed first to bury his father. I think he meant, "Let me care for my sick father who is about to die." Jesus responded that he should let the dead bury their own dead and follow Him. In Luke 18:28-30 the same thought is expressed, but with a

Birthing the Church

promise: "And Peter said, 'Behold, we have left our own homes, and followed You.' And He said to them, 'Truly I say to you, there is no one who has left house or wife or brothers or parents or children, for the sake of the kingdom of God, who shall not receive many times as much at this time and in the age to come, eternal life.' "

I can't find anyone in Scripture being warned to spend more time with family. Rather, the warning is that family must not become more important to us than ministering in the service of our Lord. I believe that in pursuing a noble goal for the restoration of the family, the body of Christ has often missed the true teaching of the Word.

My childhood memories include rough-housing with my Dad on the living room floor. They include a very special Christmas when we had no money, so Dad cut up two-by-four mill ends to make a magnificent mound of blocks for us kids. Each Christmas, before we could go see our presents, we had to eat a full breakfast—which we hardly chewed—while Mom and Dad watched with twinkling eyes. I remember sitting at Dad's feet and listening to him or Mom read Dickens to us. I learned to love working in the vegetable garden by walking barefoot next to him over the newly tilled earth. These are wonderful memories of private family time. But they are *not* the most formative or cherished memories for me, precious as they are.

What I treasure most is what I saw Mom and Dad *doing* in service to God and the way in which we kids always felt included. It was *our* ministry. I remember a time in my eighth or ninth year when we picked up a woman hitchhiker just outside Chicago while we were on

Family and Church: A Biblical Balance

---

a family vacation. She had been badly beaten. That became the occasion for a meaningful discussion on violence and compassion once we dropped her off. We were all a part of that simple act of mercy. Another time we took in an alcoholic woman to live with us while she tried to dry out. I recall that at one point she drank up the rubbing alcohol. I don't believe she ever quit, but we all participated in the ministry, and we all learned something. Many nights my father would bring home a derelict to dinner on fifteen minutes' notice to my mother, who never got used to it.

There were frequent, gentle instructions on how and why we were different from other people because of our relationship to Jesus. Therefore, we weren't supposed to hit back or curse or yell at one another or have temper tantrums or be stingy. When the troubles began at the churches Dad served, I remember he and Mom discussing it woundedly at home—sometimes with anger—but what I remember most clearly is the way they prayed, swallowed hard and went out the door to love the attackers. Sometimes Dad took me on hospital calls and visits to shut-ins. From time to time we shared prayer over a sick pet. There were midnight telephone calls asking for help, wakening the whole family. There were Christian people who loved us as if we were their own.

I was rooted in family and family was rooted in the Lord, in the church and in ministry. The center of our lives was our ministry. In that setting something was written deeply into me that I now cherish more than any of our tender, private moments.

Our family has never felt for more than a few fleeting

Birthing the Church

moments the tension between family and church that occurs when we try to live by a set of priorities that says family is to be first before ministry. For what is now two generations, Joshua 24:15 has been our balance and watchword: "... but as for me *and my house*, we will serve the Lord." God never intended family to be self-serving, existing for its own sake as an end in itself. When family is turned inward as a goal in itself, it is bound to fail. In fact, anything in life that becomes an end in itself has become an idolatry. Family *can* become an idolatry.

I have always taught that child rearing is preparation for separation. That is, we rear our children not to bind them to ourselves but to make them independent of us and able to join themselves fully to their own mates at the proper time, according to the last verse of Genesis 2. The dimension I didn't see until later, although I was reared in it and practiced it myself, is that our child rearing is training for ministry. I do that by including my children in my ministry so that our family has a goal in the Lord outside of itself toward which all of us are nurtured. We then move and succeed together with a worshipful purpose not only in our ministry, but also in our private times.

The law of God is that we can't keep what we don't give away. "He who seeks to save his life will lose it but he who loses his life for My sake and the gospel's will keep it ..." The family that gives itself away together in the service of God is the family that succeeds in love and nurture as a unit. This means that my wife is my full and equal partner. It is our ministry, not just mine with her along to help. We give *our* love away together in ministry, and

Family and Church: A Biblical Balance

together we reap God's love in return.

When I have to be gone on pastoral duties, Beth and the children pray for me and thus are involved in the ministry. The children are important, and when we can, Beth and I take them with us to the ministry in the church and on our speaking trips. I counsel in my office at home, which means that lots of folks spend lots of time in our house. My children have a sense of sharing in that ministry. By their actions and their relationship to me witnessed by others, they participate in the healing of broken people. They ask questions. They pray. They watch and absorb. When Beth and I travel to teach, we explain to our kids why we are going, and we have family prayer for the ministry we'll be doing while we're gone. When Beth and I travel, she shares the speaking, we sing together in performance, and she does a kind of interpretive mime with music that is all her own. We find that in so giving ourselves away as a partnership in love, our message is validated for our hearers, and our marriage is enriched. Often people tell us that we ourselves are the message as much as what we say.

In this regard, one of the most freeing things in my ministry happened after we had returned from a vacation. I had been working very hard all year under conditions of great stress, and I decided I needed a long vacation in order to recover my humanity. That was okay as far as it went. All work and no play makes Jack a dull boy, as the old saying goes. The first two weeks were glorious. I got back to being myself and drank deeply of the Lord's presence. The second two weeks I slipped off into the deepest, darkest depression I had ever experienced. I struggled with why and began to wonder how I could go home to the church and expect to function.

But when I stepped before my congregation, I heard God say simply and profoundly, "You are a pastor." The depression immediately lifted and I was filled with the joy of my salvation in a new way. I am not able to be a professional in one setting and a human being in another. I can't live with that sort of emotional schizophrenia. God was saying to me that "pastor" is the very definition of my being. "Pastor" is who I am, my life, my breath, my reason for living. My family—my whole family—participates in that ministry and in that identity with me. I'm told that it makes me a very warm and personal pastor as well, because I simply am who I am, pastor and person. And I will take shorter vacations in the future.

More and more, our people are catching the vision of family ministry. One couple in our church has put in a lot of time on our various building projects. Their boys, ages one and two-and-a-half, go with them to tote nails and carry away scrap. They're a lot less help than they think they are, but they're included in the ministry and that's the important thing. Families, as families, take in stray homeless ones. Couples together lead our home fellowships. Some of our best children's ministry teams are man and wife. One family is a licensed foster home for troubled teens. When there's a construction project to be completed at the church, the father brings three or four foster sons, and they work together in God's service. We are full-time Christians and that means full-time ministry for all. "Slave of Christ" is the life, breath and very being of every Christian, and our families participate in that.

Family and Church: A Biblical Balance

I have a bachelor's degree in music, and as I was studying I remember wondering why there were really no truly great artists in my field of artistic endeavor after the mid-1800's. We have not again seen the like of a Bach, a Beethoven, a Mozart or a Handel, for instance. I believe the answer lies in the effect of the industrial revolution in the late nineteenth century on family life. Prior to that time there was the family shop attached to the home. When a young person was old enough, he went to work alongside his father. In ancient Rome, a soldier took his son to train with him, the senator took his son to the senate, and so on. This gave a strength to a developing child that fostered greatness. The industrial revolution changed all that. Daddy went away to work and left the kids at home, hence we have seen no true greats in the arts since the late nineteenth century.

How can we recover that? If the family is turned outward together to minister, then we can recover that very special strength with vigor. If we can catch the vision of the family giving itself away together, we will be rearing a generation of spiritual giants whose wisdom will stand head and shoulders above our own, and that spiritual strengh will carry over into the way they pursue their studies, their jobs, their marriages and more. The simple giving act of faithful family involvement in church is a very good start with profound and far-reaching effects. How important it is for the children just to witness mom and dad being consistent and faithful in devotion to the body of Christ!

As a passing point, let me say that some of the best times I had as a child were in the nursery or the child-care program at church while my parents were at

Birthing the Church

meetings. That was holy time that I needed to spend with my peers as much as my parents needed to spend time with their peers. I think we ought not to feel guilty about nursery time for our kids. The important thing is that we went to the house of God together.

Finally, when a balance must be struck between family and ministry, I have found that God and my family provide it daily *if* I listen. My kids tell me when I have been away too much. They get tense or rebellious or both. They cry too easily. They ask hurt questions like, "Are you going to *another* meeting tonight?" Then I know I need to invest some private time at home. The church will send me the same signals from time to time, and then I ask my family to stand and sacrifice with me for a while. Simply stated, we find the balance by listening to the needs.

Let me summarize by examining Deuteronomy 6:1 and following:

> Now this is the commandment, the statutes and the judgments which the Lord your God has commanded me to teach you, that you might do them in the land where you are going over to possess it, *so that you, your son, and your grandson* might fear the Lord your God to keep all His statutes and His commandments which I command you, all the days of your life, and that your days may be prolonged.

This is a three-generational vision we are called to cultivate by the quality of our obedience. Beginning at Deuteronomy 6:6 the point is driven home more firmly:

Family and Church: A Biblical Balance

And these words which I am commanding you today shall be on your heart; and you *shall teach them diligently to your sons* and shall talk of them when you sit in your house and when you walk by the way and when you lie down and when you rise up.

Life is to be a continual act of service and obedience to God in which our children participate. Our words and our actions *are* the lesson. *Let's train our children for ministry* as we give our families away in service.

10
Burden Bearing

Luke 9:23-25
And He was saying to them all, "If anyone wishes to come after Me, let him deny himself, and take up his cross daily; and follow Me. For whoever wishes to save his life shall lose it, but whoever loses his life for My sake, he is the one who will save it. For what is a man profited if he gains the whole world, and loses or forfeits himself?"

Galatians 6:2
Bear one another's burdens, and thus fulfill the law of Christ.

Romans 15:1
Now we who are strong ought to bear the weaknesses of those without strength and not just please ourselves.

Colossians 3:12-13
And so, as those who have been chosen of God,

holy and beloved, put on a heart of compassion, kindness, humility, gentleness, and patience; bearing with one another, and forgiving each other, whoever has a complaint against anyone; just as the Lord forgave you, so also should you.

The basic work of the church, as it shares in Christ's ministry, is this thing called "burden bearing." I used to think that to give up my life in order to gain it meant to give up my selfishness and my sin in order to walk with Jesus. However, the problem with such thinking is that my selfishness and sin are my *death*, not my life. The word about giving up one's life is given in the context of the cross. The cross of Christ was and is the place where He bore the sins of others. It was the place where the sanctity and the cleanness of His personal, unique, intimate relationship with His Father was surrendered so that we could be forgiven. That relationship with His Father was His life. I believe this is the import of His cry, "My God, My God, why hast Thou forsaken Me?" (Matt. 27:46). This is no questioning cry, but one of dismay as He was sundered from His Father for the first time and suffered the fullness of hell for us so that we might be freed. In turn, our life is our relationship with Jesus. "I am the way, the truth, and *the life* . . ." (John 14:6). This may sound outrageous to some, but the life of the cross, the essence of burden bearing and of the work of the church, is to surrender the sanctity and private cleanness of our personal relationships to Jesus in order to absorb and bear the sins of others in such a way that they are set free. As the Father sent Jesus, so Jesus sends us with authority over sin (John 20:21-23).

Burden Bearing

I am speaking of a cross-centered form of intensified compassion. I can suffer *with* and *for* others and so set them free. For example, I am a minister today in large part because my mother and father could risk the cleanness of their lives in the community and in the church to absorb my teenage mess. Because there was no self-righteous condemnation of my behavior, because they simply suffered with me as I got into nearly every sort of sin imaginable and common to teenagers in the '60s, because they hurt for me and forgave me, I was able to come to them for instruction and to find God's righteousness for myself. They could have reacted to protect their position in the community as pastor and wife of the most prominent church in town, or to protect their own images of themselves, or to keep the home pure and clean, but they didn't.

At Cornerstone we had an aging hippie in our congregation, only recently converted. He had been into every sort of drug experience, especially cannabinoids, for many years. He had even been a dealer to such a degree that it became necessary to carry a concealed weapon in his vehicle. He had been poor. He had been rich. He had been abused by parents as a child. He had been divorced and remarried and divorced and remarried again. As a Christian he was growing, but he had a continuing problem with marijuana abuse and was into constant battles with his self-righteous teenage son over it. One time in the middle of an argument he said to his son, "You ain't lived long enough to say nothing to me! You don't know about where I've been! But that man," he said pointing to me, "he's been where I've been and I'll listen to him!" I'd never been a dealer. My bout with drugs

Birthing the Church

lasted a few scant months and was limited to cannabinoids (I was too afraid of the chemicals). I have never been divorced. I grew up in a wonderful home. He knew all that. He was saying I had walked with him in my heart, had borne his burden in suffering with him *before* asking him to change, and so I had the right to speak when his son did not.

One of our charter members developed breast cancer, necessitating a radical mastectomy. The Lord directed a woman parishioner and me to be by her bedside the moment she woke from the anesthesia. As soon as we were allowed in by the hospital personnel, we stood by her to pray. Both of us left the room with our hearts reeling under a sense of desolation and mutilation. The cancer victim never felt it. We had borne it for her, and so she was spared the psychological shock which commonly accompanies such an operation. A year and a half later, when her life setting and her body were settled enough to handle it, she experienced a mild period of grieving over her loss and then was free.

The essence of compassion is nonjudgmentally to absorb the sins of the sufferings of brothers and sisters. That's part of my gift in counseling. I absorb and experience in my heart what is in the heart of the other. Most counselees know, therefore, that in my inner life I have lived their trouble and experienced it, if only vicariously, and so my rebuke and exhortation can be heard.

Understand that, although each member of the body of Christ is called to share in the burden-bearing work of the church, some are called to individual ministries of burden bearing. One Sunday, knowing burden bearing to be the essence of the redemptive work of the church, I preached a message similar to this written one and called for those who wished to be burden bearers to come forward for a prayer for anointing. The result, over the next two years, was the raising up of a group of magnificent lay counselors and intercessors.

Unfortunately, the burden nearly killed them until they learned that the burdens weren't theirs at all, but the burdens of Christ *in* them. He in me bears the hurt of a brother's divorce. He in me experiences and bears the destruction of a drug abuser. He in me brings new life and deeper joy as I give my life away in the work of the cross to bear the sins of others and to let their brokenness soil my clean and peaceful little Christian corner. He *in* me is the sin bearer as well as the resurrected and resurrecting one. I can therefore give away my life, which is my cleanness and holiness in relationship to Him, in order to suffer with and for others, only to receive more life in return.

I believe this is why the Scripture says, "Sorrow is better than laughter, for when a face is sad, a heart may be happy" (Eccl. 7:3). A portion of this was in Paul's heart when he wrote that he desired "to know Him, and the power of His resurrection and the fellowship of His sufferings, being conformed to His death; in order that I may attain to the resurrection from the dead" (Phil. 3:10-11). To suffer as Christ did is to bear the sins of others. We are to die the same sort of death He died, and the result is resurrection.

In His death He bore the sins of others to redeem them. I believe that if we do our job in burden bearing, sinners will flock to fill our pews. They will come to our welcome and to our love and will be freed to change. Too many of our churches are not filled with repenting sinners because we are so busy trying to protect our comfortable, clean little corners of the world. Because they would sully and disrupt it all, sinners aren't really welcome among us. They sense our attitude and stay away.

The hard part of burden bearing is learning to let Christ bear the burden. I can't give many practical pointers in this regard, because there are no methods. Each individual learns the lesson in his or her own way. The common denominator seems to be a divinely imposed overload which defeats our fleshly ability to bear up and drives us to our Lord in helplessness. In our defeat we learn. I have yet to see a burden bearer learn to let Christ bear the burden in him by any means other than that of blessed defeat. When I have so learned that I can't bear it, not just with my mind, but in the depth of my being, then I am free to let Jesus do it in me. My fleshly ability and the desire of my sin nature to bear it all myself must be broken. Every burden bearer is first crushed, then resurrected. "All discipline for the moment seems not to be joyful, but sorrowful; yet to those who have been trained by it, afterwards it yields the peaceful fruit of righteousness" (Heb. 12:11).

By experience I have learned how to recognize which burdens are my own emotions tied to my own life and which ones are for someone else. Again, the learning can be an agony. Too many of our burden bearers got tied up again and again in emotions that confused them. They mistakenly wore them as their own, and only in defeat were they able to see that the burden really was someone else's. In this context, the simple act of

Burden Bearing

compartmentalizing helps us get the vicarious burden to the cross. Ask, "Is there any reason for me to be feeling this way?" If not, then pray accordingly for whoever it may be, even if you don't mentally know who it is. God usually reveals the individual within a day or two, along with the fruit of the praying.

I found myself one day suddenly burdened for the husband of a church member I had been counseling. I felt his desperation and anger. Two days later he told me he had hurt his back and the pain had driven him back a step or two into some old sin patterns he had been seeking to escape. Prayer kept him from falling over the precipice. I wasn't crushed by his burden because I identified the feeling as being someone else's and then praised God that I didn't have to lose my joy over it. Jesus bears it *in* me. Spirit-guided experience is the teacher. Often I am nearly crushed by feelings of despair and futility until Jesus hauls me up by the neck and makes me see that in my life I have no reason to despair. All is going well. I know then that the burden is another's, and I set about thanking God for His bearing of it in me so that I don't have to carry it to my own destruction. Having come to that conclusion, I usually discover within a matter of days that my congregation, for instance, had slipped into an agony of fear over our unemployment situation, which is staggering. Out of my knowledge that the burden is for others and that Christ bears it in me, I am able to maintain my joy while compassionately lifting those who need to be lifted.

Burden bearers must know and mentally rehearse the fact that they are not responsible for the people whose burdens they bear. Our Lord is the fruit giver. We are only servants to pray in relation to the burdens. When the heart is found to be tense, tight or angry in relation to the one for whom the burden is borne, then the burden bearer must realize that the problem is really his personal ego wanting to be puffed up by someone else's change. He must surrender that sin to Jesus and set the burdened one free.

The next point is crucial. Burden bearers must be involved in home fellowships. "Two are better than one because they have a good return for their labor. For if either of them falls, the one will lift up his companion. But woe to the one who falls when there is not another to lift him up. Furthermore, if two lie down together they keep warm, but how can one be warm alone? And if one can overpower him who is alone, two can resist him. A cord of three strands is not quickly torn apart" (Eccles. 4:9-12). If no home fellowship is available, then at the very least every burden bearer needs a prayer partner to go to for help. The most important function of that fellowship or that individual is to point the burden bearer always back to Christ. Our eyes turn too easily from Jesus to focus on the burdens so that the burdens crush the Spirit. Helpers and spiritual watchdogs can remedy that problem and even prevent it from happening.

Paul commanded that we should confront the unruly, encourage the fainthearted, help the weak, and be patient with all men (1 Thess. 5:14). He wrote that we should admonish and teach every man (Col. 1:28 and 3:12-16). In the home fellowship I have given my brothers and sisters the right to deal intimately with me for confrontation, correction and encouragement. They

Burden Bearing

watch carefully *how* I carry burdens and help me sort them out. They bear the burden of my personal sin and then confront me with it. They will keep me human by making me laugh when I get too serious. They will make me take my wife out to a movie if I am too involved in the burdens of others. They do whatever it takes to keep me balanced and free! They do this for me and they do it for one another. Our job in this regard is to make certain each of us carries only those burdens God has called him to carry.

Although bearing one another's burdens begins as a spiritual work in prayer, it demands redemptive, healing acts. I may have to hug the coldhearted, sit in a bar with a drunk, listen to an unbeliever tell dirty jokes without responding in condemnation, hear hair-raising stories of violence and murder, and experience the destruction of each of these in my heart as I speak to minister the gospel. I may need to father the fatherless and give my home to the homeless. I may be called upon to trust the untrustworthy. I will have to allow sinners to rattle my religious cage. Once a couple came to church with their German shepherd dog. It became readily apparent that if the dog didn't attend worship, neither would they; so we worshiped with a dog that day and a few times after that. We can stand to have our clean little religious corner of the world shaken up a bit. Holy forms and places are always secondary to the needs of people.

When I was serving in Sacramento, an eighteen-year-old was being neglected by the college group leaders and everyone else too. When I brought this to the attention of the leaders, one angrily responded, "All he ever wants to talk about is cars. I don't want to hear about cars! I am not interested in cars!" I said, "Then you become interested in cars and you buy the right to speak the gospel. If you have to listen to car talk for six hours to get five minutes of gospel time, you do it!"

I have been known to spend long hours after midnight in a hospital emergency room holding a "barf bucket" for an OD'd alcoholic just to buy a moment of love and trust. At first, for many of us in Cornerstone, these burdens and acts of mercy only drained energy. Many trudged on obediently, staggering under the load, and hating every moment of it, until, in defeat, it was written on the heart that *Jesus* is the bearer *in* us. When that lesson is learned, an entirely different kind of energy flows into the ministry which I can only characterize with the word, "peace."

"Therefore, since Christ has suffered in the flesh," to absorb our sin and so free us, "arm yourselves also with the same purpose," by bearing the sin and suffering of others in yourself in order to redeem" (1 Pet. 4:1). Compassion buys the right to minister.

11
Pentecost Power

As I grew up in the charismatic movement when it was making inroads into the mainline denominations, I struggled with the model our movement presented for the baptism in the Spirit. I remember what tremendous pressure there was to speak in tongues. The idea was—and too often still is—that one has not been baptized in the Spirit until he speaks in tongues. I remember one particularly frightening moment when hands were laid on me for prayer, and I was pressured by the group to speak in tongues on the spot. I couldn't and I went away crushed and discouraged, feeling like a second-class citizen in the Kingdom. Seven years later, in my seminary years, God led me into tongues. His timing!

Many others have had similar high-pressure experiences and in some cases have walked away from the movement altogether. Already, before the first hair sprouted on my face, I had been charbroiled in the furnace of division that resulted when some brothers and sisters began to feel looked-down-upon by the "we-have-it-and-you-don't" crowd. Granted, division will

Birthing the Church

always result when some want to move on in the Spirit and others don't. But still, it seemed to me that a greater degree of disharmony existed than ought to. Applying the principle that bad fruit can't come from a good tree and knowing beyond a doubt that the charismatic movement was, indeed, of God, I set out to find the scriptural source for our teaching on the Holy Spirit. What I found is the basis of what I teach at Cornerstone regarding the baptism in the Spirit, and it has enabled us to carry a loving and open witness to our denomination without encountering any of the fireworks I witnessed while growing up. I believe it stands the test of Scripture, neither adding to nor detracting from the Word of God, and it passes the test of fruit inspection.

Let me begin with some simple Christian distinctives.

1. God is a trinity, three persons, but one God.
2. The second person of that Trinity was incarnate and made man.
3. That second person died for me and rose again so that I might live.
4. The third person of the Trinity is the Holy Spirit who was in Christ and now manifests himself to us as the Spirit of Christ. He is the presence of Christ in me in Christ's physical absence (John 14:16-18 and Rom. 8:9-11).
5. Therefore, it is Christ's Spirit, Christ himself, who indwells me by faith. According to 1 Corinthians 12:3, that occurred at the moment of my confession of Jesus as Lord. In fact, it is the Spirit who enabled and enables that confession.

What is it then, to be baptized in the Spirit? I believe that as we have overindividualized our faith and expression in every other area of our walk with Christ, so we have overindividualized our understanding of the baptism in the Spirit. We speak of that baptism as being something primarily personal when, in fact, Scripture never records an individual experience of that kind. Joel 2:28 teaches, "I will pour out my Spirit on *all* mankind . . . ." The very distinctive of the new age in Christ was prophesied to be that *all* believers would be empowered and indwelt by the Spirit. The age of selective indwelling, when some such as prophets and judges were anointed and others were not, ended on the day of Pentecost when Joel 2:28 was fulfilled and confirmed by Peter in his Pentecost sermon (Acts 2). There can be no un-Spirit-baptized Christians in the new age. All partake, but not all speak in tongues according to 1 Corinthians 12, at least not right away. Tongues are one sign, not the only sign, of Spirit baptism. In Acts 2 *all* 120 in the upper room were filled and empowered.

Peter affirmed in Acts 2:38 and 39 that *whoever* repented and was baptized would certainly receive the gift of the Holy Spirit, in the fullness of Pentecost, according to the context, and that the promise was for *as many as* would believe from generation to generation. Acts 8 reports the Samaritans believing and receiving the Holy Spirit. It seems, again, to be a corporate experience with none left out. In Acts 10 Peter was preaching to Cornelius's household, and the Holy Spirit fell upon them *all*.

So, to be baptized in the Spirit is to come into a corporate experience so profound the disciples refer to it

Birthing the Church

as "the beginning" (Acts 11:15-17). *All* who believe have the Spirit. John 20:22-23 records the giving of the Spirit for dealing with sin. I see this giving as an individual thing for individual cleansing and for individual ministry and forgiveness. 1 Corinthians 12:3 speaks of that individual indwelling which makes us able to confess Jesus as Lord. But these aren't yet the baptism in the Spirit in the historical progression, because the baptism in the Spirit is corporate. It happens to groups, to the body of Christ, but to individuals only by virtue of the fact that they are part of the body of Christ. I am baptized in the Spirit because in Christ I am part of the church and am a member of that one body. We are a *nation* of priests, a holy *people* for God's own possession.

Often one who has been ignorant of or locked up from the fullness of the Spirit's power breaks through suddenly into a new and fuller experience. If we hold to the old teaching, we say that at that moment he was baptized in the Spirit. I say he came into a fuller experience of what was already his by virtue of his membership in the body of Christ, and it is the body of Christ that was and is baptized in the Holy Spirit. We found that when we make the baptism in the Holy Spirit not a matter of the "haves" and the "have nots" but a matter of the "free" and the "not so free," then we have a much lessened problem with disunity and rejection. We say, "All believers have it, but not all avail themselves of it or are released in it."

Biblical baptism in the Spirit is first an immersion. The Greek *baptizo* means immersion. Therefore, we are not only filled individually, but immersed corporately. Jesus baptized, or immersed, the church as a corporate entity into the Spirit. Jesus is the baptizer. The Spirit is the medium of baptism. Thus John the Baptist's prophecy for the corporate body was fulfilled: "He Himself will baptize you with the Holy Spirit and fire" (Matt. 3:11). For individuals the Spirit is the baptizer and the body of Christ is the medium of baptism. "For *by* one Spirit we were *all* baptized *into* one body . . ." (1 Cor. 12:13). By the Spirit I am immersed individually into the body of Christ, which is corporately immersed in the Spirit by virtue of the day of Pentecost.

At this point it is necessary to make a distinction. What happened on the day of Pentecost was, indeed, the beginning for the whole church in every age. In the same way that all of us are already made righteous in Christ by virtue of His death and resurrection—although we have to work that out in the process of sanctification—so the whole church is baptized and empowered in the Spirit by virtue of the day of Pentecost. Yet each local congregation must come into its own corporate Pentecost in its own way at its own time. It must work out in reality what it already possesses in principle. I have seen churches full of empowered, tongues-speaking believers that had no power as churches. Why? Each congregation needs its own corporate Pentecost. We can come into Pentecost power individually as members of dead churches because the power of the Spirit given in Acts 2 is for the whole body with all its members. The whole church, in principle, was anointed that day. We individually partake of that corporate anointing. Yet, each local congregation needs to seek that empowering for its own corporate life and work. It needs a corporate immersion. When a local body is baptized or immersed in the Spirit in its life together, then I who am filled with the Spirit become surrounded by, carried by and immersed in the Spirit in an even greater fullness.

For many months in Cornerstone I wrestled with how we could have so many members walking with Pentecost power in their individual lives and yet have so little Pentecost power in our corporate life. God led us to begin praying for a literal Pentecost to descend on our corporate life. We all expected a mighty wind, an earthquake and tongues of fire on our heads. It never came. What did come was a new awareness and a gradual increase in the occurrence and significance of signs and wonders, a progressive deepening of our sense of discipleship and responsibility, and an increase in our growth rate. What happened to the 120 in a day happened to us over a period of time. God meets each congregation individually and appropriately.

We found that a body which seeks its corporate Pentecost must first expect a burning and a purging according to John the Baptist's word in Matthew 3:11. That implies a single-minded seeking after personal and corporate holiness.

John 20:21-23 reads:

> Jesus therefore said to them again, "Peace be with you; as the Father has sent Me, I also send you." And when He had said this, He breathed on them, and said to them, "Receive the Holy Spirit. If you forgive the sins of any, their sins have been forgiven them; if you retain the sins of any, they have been retained."

Pentecost Power

This is the first work of the Spirit in preparation for power. He comes to cleanse and deal with sin and thereby complete the work of the cross. We have, by virtue of John 20:21-23, been given authority over sin in what I see to be four ways.

1. We have the *authority of absolution.* For the benefit of heart knowledge, and to break the power of guilt in a life, we have the power to say, "In the name of Jesus, I forgive you for _____." Guilts from alcoholism, sexual sin, judgments held and exercised, lying, and so on, can all be healed by this simple statement in prayer following upon confession and repentance. Guilty saints tend not to walk in power.

2. We have the *authority of reconciliation.* When disunity has prevailed, we need to look one another in the eye and say clearly, "I forgive you," or, "I'm sorry, will you forgive me?"

3. We have the *authority of admonition* (Rom. 15:14) to catch one another in sin and unrighteousness, and to confront one another to repentance and change.

4. We have *authority to heal the bitter root.* "Pursue peace with all men, and the sanctification without which no one will see the Lord. See to it that no one comes short of the grace of God; that no root of bitterness springing up causes trouble, and by it many be defiled . . ." (Heb. 12:14-15). The bitter root is any unclean expectation of life and persons which can stem from unhealthy past or present reactions to parents or others. Whatever we have judged mother and father for doing or being, that we will most certainly reap (Eph. 6:1-3), even trapping those who would treat us righteously into treating us unrighteously. We can identify destructive patterns in

our lives, trace them to roots of judgment, deal with them in repentance, forgiveness and healing prayer, and so come to holiness. Please read *The Transformation of the Inner Man* by John and Paula Sandford for detailed instruction on this word about bitter roots. My point here is that we are not stuck in our sin and our troubles. We *can* grow. There *is* more. Jesus has given to us the tools with which to move from where we are to where He wants us to be.

So, the message of John 20:21-23 as it prepares us for Pentecost is to minister to one another until the house is clean. Ground one another in love, and don't be surprised or dismayed by the trouble that may result as Pentecost approaches. Cleansing comes with fire and fire often involves pain. Pain in turn ignites rebellion. Ugly hatreds and angers may surface; disagreements may explode out of proportion; sin will be revealed to be sin; and all because God is calling us to cleanliness, joy and power.

To sum up our authority over sin, *forgiveness given* says that God and I will treat you as if you had never offended, even knowing that you will offend again. When *applied* and *received*, forgiveness says that the power of sin is now broken and rooted out of individual and/or corporate life. The reaping of its consequences is taken to the cross. Pentecost power cannot come wholesomely and cleanly to an individual or fellowship still living in the spiritual outhouse. If it did, we'd mess it all up, like my six-year-old son driving my sports car at ninety miles an hour into a wall. God must cleanse us before we can safely be trusted with power.

I once complained to the Lord that my spiritual life

Pentecost Power

was so stable. "Why don't I get translated to heaven, carried away in my emotions, and slain in the Spirit like other people, Lord?" His answer came as a question. "Would you rather have foolish power or powerful wisdom?" I made a choice I've never regretted. First the cleansing, then the power. I have seen God give power to a baby too soon because His people bugged Him to do so for so long that He gave in and said, "Learn the hard way," and the hard way always resulted. Sheep were destroyed when gifts were misused and misunderstood by unclean hearts. Spirit and fire belong together, but fire comes first.

The second thing John the Baptist expected, and which comes together with cleansing, was a great ingathering and separating. When we decided in favor of holiness and obedience at Cornerstone, a large faction left the church. God will have clean hearts. He simply drove out those who would not be cleansed. Any church in renewal must reconcile itself to the fact that not all will respond to the movement of the Spirit. Many will react aggressively and some will leave the church. There will be an unavoidable showdown at some point. Those who left us didn't leave over the issue of the Spirit. All were "charismatics" already. They left because there was no longer a place for the destruction which their sin brought to our body and because they refused repentance and self-examination when the showdown came. Those who stayed became whole and found peace.

After the appearance to the disciples on resurrection day, the Lord remained with them forty days and forty nights until, ten days before Pentecost, He ascended, leaving instructions as recorded in Acts 1:4-5 and 7-8,

Birthing the Church

that they should remain in Jerusalem and wait for the promised power. Verses 12-14 indicate that they retired to the upper room and began to pray until, ten days later, 120 were gathered in great unity (Acts 2:1).

I believe they prayed continually for ten days, and I believe that by virtue of John 20:21-23 the time was devoted to rooting out and repenting for sin. Perhaps John and James asked forgiveness for wanting to be first in the Kingdom, and the others granted it, asking forgiveness in return for being angry with them over it. Perhaps Peter repented of being an arrogant big mouth, confessing his weakness and his denial of the Lord on crucifixion eve. I know for certain what a backlog of confession they had to catch up on after three years together, and how deeply aware of his weaknesses each would be after the pain of the crucifixion. They dealt with sin those ten days. When they were clean, whole and *together*, God gave power, and 3,000 were converted in a day.

My first charge as a pastor was to develop the youth program at Hope United Methodist Church in Sacramento. A few months after I arrived, I decided we needed a breakthrough. The Lord led me to gather all fifteen of our kids into my office to pray by candlelight. That was a risk. They had never prayed well before, and I couldn't see why they would begin then. I told them we would sit in silence for several hours if it took that, but we were going to pray one way or another. I called it a "mystery meeting" just to get them there because I knew they'd never come just to pray. We began at 7 P.M., and we were out of words by 7:15 P.M. We sat until 9 P.M. in silence. Suddenly a girl jumped up, ran to her brother, embraced him, and asked forgiveness for hating him and always treating him wrongly. The whole group dissolved into tears as one kid after another repented of interpersonal hatreds, judgments on parents, moral sins, and simple religious apathy. Within three months our group of fifteen was a group of seventy. In the next two years we were to see a number of miraculous healings come from that fellowship, and several of the young men went on to full-time professional Christian service. Prayer marathons became a favorite event for those kids.

The year after God moved in Cornerstone to cleanse and to separate, our growth rate was 50 percent with no evangelism program. In the same year, stewardship giving jumped 60 percent. We saw internal injuries healed by prayer on the eve of scheduled surgery. An anonymous outside donor stepped up to pour funds into our new building. Our home fellowships began to work. The people began to volunteer freely for the various tasks of the church, and ministry began to be fun! Lives changed. Marriages were healed. The youth group doubled in size under lay leadership. We began to move!

Pentecost will happen for any individual or group that decides to take up its authority, quit making excuses for sin, and deal with it head on. We are not stuck with our sinful condition. For freedom Christ has set us free.

When the power comes, let us recognize that it is never personal, on account of "me," but the corporate power of the church as the Holy Spirit empowered the whole church on the day of Pentecost, and as that power is renewed to each local congregation that seeks it and pays the price for it.

I close with an ending that is a beginning. For too

Birthing the Church

many of us in the charismatic movement Pentecost is the goal and there we stop, as if in living out the gifts of the Spirit we have somehow "arrived." Pentecost is no more than a birth, a starting place. The year 1982 saw the birth of Cornerstone as a church, as a solid, viable force for the Lord's work. The mission now begins. Now we make disciples. Now we look to the building of the lay counseling center, staffed by trained lay people and offered to the community. Now we begin to be a force for renewal and for change in our community as we send our people to minister in their various niches outside the church. Now we can become more concerned for the plight of the physically and spiritually poor beyond our circle than we are about our own problems. Now we put meat on the bones of our vision, and we do it in power and in victory.